GLORY, JEST AND RIDDLE

GLORY, JEST AND RIDDLE

A Study of the Growth of Individualism
from Homer to Christianity

J. D. P. BOLTON

BOOKS
10 East 53d St., New York 10022
(a division of Harper & Row Publishers, Inc.)

Published in the U.S.A. 1973 by Harper & Row Publishers, Inc.
Barnes & Noble Import Division

© 1973 J. D. P. Bolton

ISBN 06 490578 0

Printed in Great Britain by Bristol Typesetting Company Limited
Barton Manor, St Philips, Bristol

LIBERIS CONIUGIQUE CARISSIMIS

καὶ ἔλαβον τὸ βιβλαρίδιον ἐκ τῆς χειρὸς τοῦ ἀγγέλου, καὶ κατέφαγον αὐτό. καὶ ἦν ἐν τῷ στόματί μου ὡς μέλι γλυκύ, καὶ ὅτε ἔφαγον αὐτό, ἐπικράνθη ἡ κοιλία μου.

Plac'd on this isthmus of a middle state,
A being darkly wise, and rudely great:
With too much knowledge for the Sceptic side,
With too much weakness for the Stoic's pride,
He hangs between; in doubt to act, or rest;
In doubt to deem himself a God, or Beast;
In doubt his Mind or Body to prefer;
Born but to die, and reas'ning but to err;
Alike in ignorance, his reason such,
Whether he thinks too little, or too much:
Chaos of Thought and Passion, all confus'd;
Still by himself abus'd, or disabus'd;
Created half to rise, and half to fall;
Great Lord of all things, yet a prey to all;
Sole judge of Truth, in endless Error hurl'd:
The glory, jest and riddle of the world!

From ALEXANDER POPE'S *Essay on Man*

Preface

This book is an attempt to illuminate 'the Christian message' from an unusual – if not a novel – angle. That with Jesus the world made a new beginning is accepted as an article of faith by Christians, and as a convenience of dating by most of the rest. Christians also see him (as he saw himself) as completing or fulfilling Jewish law and prophecy. But it is also possible to see him as the culmination of a process which had been going on for centuries in the Greek, or hellenised, world into which he was born; a world which in some of its spiritual features remarkably resembled our own today. It is not really surprising that his gospel was heard more readily by Gentiles than by Jews.

Insofar as I adopt this approach, my book might seem to offer a contribution to the history of ideas: on the contrary, it is intended to contribute an idea to history. The attentive reader will (I hope) see this idea unfolding, as if he were watching a painting grow on canvas; in its fullness it is meant to give pertinence and immediacy to the belief that Jesus's life and teaching formed a keystone in the human spirit's development. By many of those who grasp it it will be found strange, eccentric, or even grotesque; if any find it also cheering and enlivening, and are moved to look again at the New Testament, I shall have been amply compensated – doubly so, if they also wish to make closer acquaintance with the Greek and Latin classics.

The best things in this book have been written by other people, and I confess my indebtedness, and my gratitude, to all, ancient or modern, whose words or ideas I have laid under contribution. The translations from the classics are mostly my own; where I have used those of others, this is acknowledged in the notes at the end of the book. It seemed prudent to assume no knowledge of Greek or Latin in the reader; as a result I must often appear to underestimate his or her learning, for which I ask pardon. I use repeatedly a few Greek words which have no adequate single English word corresponding to them; a tiresome necessity.

Contents

I

The Heroic Self

Considerate la vostra semenza:
Fatti non foste a viver come bruti,
Ma per seguir virtute e canoscenza.

'Consider the seed from which you are sprung: you were
not made to live like the dumb beasts, but to pursue excellence
(*virtute*) and knowledge.'

This was the 'little speech' with which Dante's Ulysses inspired
his comrades, though ageing now and weary with exploring the
inner sea, to press on unflaggingly into the wastes of the western
ocean. His insatiable urge to know more had overcome the love
he felt for home and son, the duty he had to his old father, the
joy he owed to his faithful Penelope. So on they went, through
the Straits of Gibraltar, those pillars set up by Hercules, greatest
of explorers, to mark the permitted limits of man's inquisitive-
ness, into the tumbling Atlantic, then south into strange seas
and nights beneath unknown stars.

There we will leave them for the moment, and look more
closely at their leader's words. With his exhortation to the men
who had fought beside him at Troy to remember the seed from
which they were sprung, Ulysses appears at first to be making a
commonplace appeal to noblemen to honour the valour of their
fathers by matching it. But the next lines show that he is
appealing, not to family pride, but to the stock of all mankind:
man's origin guarantees his end, which is not to live the un-
reasoning life of the beasts of the field, but to seek after 'excellence and knowledge' at all costs.

It is a philosophy of man against which moderns have reacted,
stressing his animal nature, his oneness with, rather than his
distinction from, the dumb beasts. Whence these ideas of

'nature', 'end' or 'natural purpose', 'excellence' or 'virtue'? What is it all about? No one talks aimless nonsense willingly, and that includes our forbears: what is the sense behind these words? To find out, we must travel back another two thousand years before Dante's time, into seas which many nowadays will find as strange as those which confronted Ulysses and his men: to the world of the original of Dante's Ulysses – Homer's Odysseus – and the Trojan War, and the beginnings of European literature.

Homer's epic of the *Iliad*, long though it is, has as its theme only one incident in the war which Paris caused between Greece and Troy. Paris, the son of the Trojan king Priam, had repaid the hospitality of the Greek Menelaus by stealing the affections of his host's wife Helen, and taking her home with him across the Aegean sea. To avenge this Agamemnon, the brother of Menelaus, from his stronghold of Mycenae in a nook of the Argive plain called for the assembly of a great armament under the command of himself with the other warlords of Greece – Diomedes, old Nestor, wily Odysseus, the two Ajaxes and, youngest and bravest of all, Achilles with his Myrmidons and his friend Patroclus.

So, from their camp on the shore of the Dardanelles at the edge of the windswept plain of Troy, they laid siege for ten years to the city, whose fate was so long postponed chiefly by the prowess of Priam's eldest son Hector, and the support of some of the Olympian gods and goddesses, who had divided their favours between the two sides, even though it was the will of their father Zeus that Troy should perish.

In the tenth year of the war the Greek enterprise nearly foundered on a bitter quarrel between Agamemnon and Achilles, whose captive, the girl Briseis, Agamemnon took from him. The *Iliad* relates the consequences of this slight: Achilles's withdrawal from the battlefield and his obstinate refusal to come to the Greeks' aid when because of his absence they were almost routed by the Trojans; how this sulkiness led to the death of Patroclus at Hector's hand; and how grief for the loss of his friend goaded Achilles back into the fray, more terrible than ever, to slay the chivalrous Hector and then to savage his body.

In Homer's world, where a man might have as his friend or

adversary a god, disguised or invisible, the men themselves – or rather the foremost of men and women, the heroes and heroines – have themselves something godlike about them. The lovely Helen is 'terribly like one of the immortal goddesses to look upon'; a stone which 'two modern men could scarcely lever on to a wagon' Hector wields as easily as if it were a woollen fleece; Achilles 'leaps the distance of a spear's throw like a swooping eagle', and his mere trumpet-roar of rage after the news of Patroclus's death is enough to send the triumphant Trojans scurrying back to safety. Yet in original fact these heroes were men of flesh and blood, no more superhuman than the poet who sang of them.

The *Iliad* and the *Odyssey* were composed, in pretty much the form in which we now have them, between about 750 and 650 BC. But their stories are set in an age five hundred years before that, near the end of the Mycenaean civilisation. Though this civilisation preceded recorded history, the kernel of the *Iliad* at least is historical. There *was* a Trojan War, and the ruins of Troy and of the cities of her Greek enemies have been uncovered. It is probable enough that Agamemnon and at any rate some of his companions were real men. More than this: such were the circumstances of the creation of the Homeric poems that, sophisticated as they are in many ways, they yet preserve relics of the culture of a much earlier, pre-literary time.

Though Agamemnon's Mycenaean contemporaries could write, their script was nothing like the classical Greek alphabet, and its use seems to have been confined to the listing of inventories by a professional secretariat. With the downfall of the Mycenaean civilisation before the inroads of the uncouth Dorian Greeks from the north, in the generations following the Trojan War, this art of writing was lost, until the eighth century BC, when the Greeks adopted and adapted the Phoenician alphabet, which they had discovered through the renewal of commerce with the Middle East. But, although during these 'Dark Ages' there was no written poetry, there were poets, repositories of an oral tradition of myth and saga, which they could reproduce in extemporary verse when called upon to do so.

They could do this with fluency because they were masters of an enormous repertoire of verbal formulae, varying in length from short phrases to several lines, which could be joined together in various combinations, or filled out, to express what the poet intended, without hesitation yet without infringing the rules of the metre. The knowledge of these formulae was probably acquired in apprenticeship at bardic schools, where over the centuries new phrases were added to old, and the total stock multiplied. The *Iliad* and *Odyssey* are packed with such formulae, and from them we can sometimes get hints of a religion, a psychology and a society more primitive than the poet's own.

Homer has often been praised for his 'rational' attitude to religion; for giving his deities human shapes and feelings, and for playing down the supernatural in his poems. But traces of other beliefs are to be found there too; less rational beliefs, some might call them – though perhaps the grading of rationality is not quite so simple.

Homer hardly mentions the Arcadians. Yet they were a far older people than he; older than the moon, men said. An uncanny people, with a primitive, pastoral culture, an island in the centre of the Peloponnese washed about by the tide of Dorian invaders; and they had an uncanny god, Pan, whose features were half human and half bestial – a blend of his shepherd worshippers and their goats. The sound of his noonday piping could induce lewd dreams in the drowsy, but the sight of him, panic fear. He was slow to leave the wooded uplands of his remote home, and we do not meet him among the Olympian gods of the *Iliad* and the *Odyssey*.

Yet in a number of passages in these poems gods or goddesses exchange their normal human shape for animal. Hermes, carrying a message from Olympus to Odysseus on Calypso's isle, skims over the waves in the likeness of the bird *laros*. On one occasion Athena leaps down from heaven like another bird, 'the shrill-voiced, long-winged *harpe*'. Hypnos (Sleep) perches on the tallest tree on Mount Ida above Troy 'like to the bird which the gods call *chalcis* and men *kumindis*'. And there is an often-repeated formulaic phrase, 'owl-faced Athena'.

A further link between gods and animals is preserved in another formula: Hera, the wife of Zeus, is called 'cow-faced'. An earlier generation of scholars, convinced of the rationality and propriety of the Greeks, was so shocked that such an epithet

4

could be applied to the queen of heaven that they wanted it to mean 'mild-eyed' – and to render the owl-face of Athena, the sagacious, embattled virgin, as 'grey-eyed'. Probably the truth is that we have here, in these formulae and bird-shapes, relics of an age when men were hardly conscious of a distinction between them and their fellow-creatures; when even the boundary of bodily form was vague, and in imagination could credibly be crossed and re-crossed by gods, and by humans too. The theme is common in folk-tale, and is perhaps presented in some of the earliest specimens of pictorial art: in the prancing figures compounded of horned animals and human limbs among the palaeolithic sketches from Ariège and the Dordogne, and the bird-headed man of Lascaux.

Another curious formula may be a sort of psychological fossil, and have its remote origin in an early stage of emergent consciousness, before the individual has formed a clear notion of the limit between himself and his environment. Quite often parts of a person's body, instead of being called 'his' or 'hers', are characterised by an adjective which can mean either 'dear' or 'friendly'. For instance, Achilles says he will never forget the dead Patroclus 'while I am among the living and dear (*or* friendly) knees stir for me'. He means, of course, his own knees; it is a grand epic way of saying 'while I am alive and kicking'. The modern rationalist would opt for the rendering 'dear': obviously his own knees are dear to their owner, and therefore they can be called 'dear' instead of 'his'. But the truth may be stranger than reason.

The idea that a man *owns* the parts of his body is not a simple idea; it is not obvious to infants or to some deranged people, who have to reach it through the discovery that certain features of the environment ('their' arms or legs) respond to their wishes – react to them in a *friendly* way.

Let a grown (modern) man stand for all those babies we may have watched in the process of discovering how their hands and feet co-operate with them. The Reverend Thomas Hanna was stunned by a heavy fall. When he recovered consciousness after several hours it was as if he were a new-born infant, opening its eyes on the world for the first time. 'Movement alone attracted his attention. He did not know the cause and meaning of

5

movement, but a moving object fastened his involuntary attention and seemed to fascinate his gaze. He made as yet no discrimination between his own movements and those of other objects, and was as much interested in the movement of his own limbs as in that of external things . . . From the more or less involuntary chance movements made by his arms and legs he learnt the possibility of controlling his limbs.' He made no spatial or temporal distinctions: shorter or longer, farther or nearer, at first meant nothing to him. And he understood no language. Yet his intelligence was brisk, and quick to learn; so quick that he mastered a banjo – an entirely new accomplishment for him – in a few hours.

If the case of the Reverend Mr Hanna be allowed to exemplify, in a striking though general way, the discovery of any human being that it is a physical unity, the myth of the Trickster does as much for the whole human race, for its hero (or anti-hero) is man himself, and its theme his emergence into self-awareness.

It was a very simple culture, that of the Winnebago Indians, which produced this story of man's learning to differentiate himself from his surroundings. 'The trickster starts as an unselfconscious, amorphous being. As the story unfolds he gradually discovers his own identity, gradually recognises and controls his own anatomical parts . . . and finally learns to assess his environment for what it is.' He is at the mercy of impulses over which he has no control; his limbs have wills of their own, even if he has none. When he was cutting up the carcase of a buffalo with a knife in his right hand 'suddenly his left arm grabbed the buffalo. "Give that back to me, it is mine! Stop that, or I will use my knife on you!" So spoke the right arm . . . Thereupon the left arm released its hold.' It may be remarked that modern behaviourists are expressing themselves in a way not unlike the Winnebago myth, when in unguarded moments they speak of men as if they were machines or puppets, but personify the same men's component cells, which 'select stimuli to which to react', or 'send messages in a chemical code', or 'go wild'.

When the boundaries of the self and the non-self are so vague, these boundaries may be (to our way of thinking) either over-narrowly constricted or over-widely extended. The Trickster's autonomous arms exemplify the former, while the latter has been noticed in some less sophisticated peoples of the present day: Iris Murdoch remarks in the heroes of certain African tales 'their fluid connection with their surroundings, the absence of a hard defining line of personality, as if it were unclear to the person himself where he ended and where the animals, trees and ancestors began'.

To most of us – differentiated, sophisticated, alienated (from whatever it is) – this seems very strange. To us our 'selves' seem self-evident, the one rock of certainty in a swirling fog; though pressure for further definition may lead to uncertainty and anxiety. In fact, as J. A. C. Brown says, 'on the face of it nothing appears to be more obvious than the fact that we are real personalities sharply distinguishable from our surrounding environment; yet such a state did not always exist in the course of our development, and it has long been known that in the mystic state or under the influence of certain drugs the boundaries of self spread far beyond their usual narrow framework leading to a feeling of "one-ness" with the universe . . . The concept of a real and enduring self is not innate but arises in the course of development and relating ourselves to our social and material environment.' This last is a continuing process, which if arrested can lead to profound mental disturbance. Brown quotes a report 'that merely taking away from a healthy university student for a few days the usual sights, sounds and bodily contact can shake him right down to the base, can disturb his personal identity, so that he is aware of two bodies (one hallucinatory), and cannot say which is his own, or perceives his personal self as vague and ill-defined; something separate from his body, looking down on where it is lying on the bed, and can disturb his capacity for critical judgment, making him eager to listen to and believe any sort of preposterous nonsense.'

On the strength of all this I believe that Achilles's legs were *friendly*, not *dear*, to him, and that the old Homeric formula hints at a stage in the growth of the psychology of our species which was as little comprehended by Homer's classical successors (perhaps by Homer himself as well) as it is by us today; for they virtually dropped the usage.

The notion of the unity of one's self marches with the notion of the unity of one's body: this friendly corporation (if I may so put it) is ultimately seen as being the self, or belonging to it. Further evidence that this notion of the unity of the self was still only half-formed in the period of the Homeric poems may be seen in the absence from them of any word for the living body. The word which later Greeks used generically for *body*, in Homer means 'corpse'. We see a man's body as his main feature, the core or centre of him, and his head and limbs as appendages to it; but to Homer the significant things about a man were his limbs, especially his hands and his knees, wherein particularly his strength seems to lie. A hero's hands are said to be invincible, while his knees carry him swiftly into and out of battle, as if they were entities separate from their owner, like the Winnebago Trickster's arms. These centres of strength are 'loosed' in death or faintness. They are the man – 'the strength of Telemachus' or 'the Heraclean might' can stand as phrases for 'Telemachus' and 'Heracles'; the body is a scarcely remarkable link between the limbs.

As a man's physical powers are located in his hands and knees, so his mental powers are located in another organ, his lungs. Indeed, his lungs and his mental powers are not at first distinguished from each other, for they are both called the same, *phrenes*. A man deliberates in, or with, his *phrenes*. The dead have no *phrenes*, except the seer Teiresias (whose ghost in the underworld kept its *phrenes* and its power to prophesy).

The lungs are the seat of a most important entity, the *thymos*. This too was probably to begin with a material object, a hot vapour (which we can perceive when we exhale). But it has a psychological aspect, for it constitutes the man's vitality, his urge to act both generally and in specific ways: it may bid him to make love to Helen, or to go hunting, or to do *something* – anything rather than just sit still and die of inanition. There is no one English word to catch its connotations exactly; 'drive' perhaps most satisfactorily gives its hint of biological impulse to action. The permanent inactivity of death is caused, or accompanied, by a final dissipation of the man's *thymos*. When he is too weary to move, his *thymos* is said to be overcome, but as it collects again in his chest his energies revive. When the Greeks surround the body of Patroclus with the single-minded intent to save it from the Trojan enemy, they are said all 'to have one

8

thymos'. Conversely, the *thymos* of a retreating and demoralised army is 'divided': it has no common purpose.

A man's *thymos* is friendly to him, like his hands and knees; like them, it is often treated as something distinct from him. Sarpedon, leader of Troy's Lycian allies, assaults the Greeks like a hungry lion whose lordly *thymos* bids him seek his prey even in the security of their farmstead, and the *thymos* is frequently said to 'command' a man in this way. When Odysseus is imprisoned in the Cyclops's cave, and thinks to slay the ogre in his sleep, a second *thymos* restrains him. And in moments of indecision or doubt a hero may address his 'great-hearted *thymos*' and debate with it what he should do.

The *thymos*, then, is that in a man which both makes him act and directs his activity. In time, he comes to own it, but at first it was treated as something extraneous to the man himself.

What moves Homeric man as an individual is *thymos*, which is ultimately a basic urge towards preservation and procreation; not self-preservation so much as the preservation of the potential of procreation. What moves him as a member of society is ultimately traceable to the same urge.

The society depicted in the Homeric poems (especially in the *Iliad*) is not far removed from that primitive society of the familial group, always liable to sudden attack by outside foes; the survival of which depends on the valour of its warriors and the stoutness of its defensive walls. Any day of your life you might be raided, robbed, kidnapped, killed; the hungry stranger you were now entertaining might turn out to be a pirate.

It was in this manner that Hector's wife Andromache had lost her father and her seven brothers in one day, as she reminds her husband when she meets him as he is about to go out to battle. The tenderness of the scene is enhanced by the wild background against which it is set. It contains the essence of the poet's code and outlook.

When Hector had reached the Scaean Gate, where he was to go out to the battlefield, his wife came running to meet him, the princess Andromache, daughter of Eetion the king of the Cilicians; and with her came a maidservant clasping to her breast Hector's dear son, who was lovely as a star, in the innocence of childhood. Hector used to call him Scamandrius, but the other Trojans called him Astyanax, Lord of the City, for without his father Hector Troy would have no protection.

Hector looked at his son in silence, smiling; but Andromache stood by him, and put her hand on him and said: 'Dear one, your strength will be the death of you, and you have no pity on your baby child or your unlucky wife, who will lose you before long; for the Greeks will set on you all together, and will soon kill you. And as for me, a grave would be best for me once I have lost you, for there will be no other comfort for me when you are dead, only sorrows. I have no father now, nor mother to look after me, for godlike Achilles when he sacked the city of the Cilicians, Thebes of the tall gates, killed my father Eetion, and my brothers, all seven of them – in a great sacrifice he killed shambling oxen and white sheep, and then my brothers. My mother he brought here as a captive with our possessions, and took a ransom for her, and she died in her father's house. Hector, *you* are father to me now, yes and brother too, as well as being my strong husband. So pity me and stay here on the battlements, and do not make your child an orphan and your wife a widow.'

Great Hector of the gleaming helmet replied: 'I think of these things too, wife; but how ashamed I should be before the Trojans, men and women, if I were to skulk like some good-for-nothing at a safe distance from the fighting. And my spirit (*thymos*) too forbids it, for I have been brought up always to play the man amongst the foremost Trojan warriors, and win great glory for my father and myself.

'I know this for certain. The day will come which will destroy Troy, destroy Priam and the people of Priam of the good ashen spear. But it is not the thought of the distress awaiting the Trojans that pains me, or that awaiting my mother Hecuba herself or king Priam, or my brothers, when many a good fighter will bite the dust at the enemy's hand, so much as your grief, when some one of the bronze-coated Achaeans leads you weeping into captivity. Then in Argos perhaps you will weave at another woman's loom, and fetch water from the spring, not because you want to but because you must. And they will say, as they see your tears, "That was the wife of Hector, who was the bravest of the horse-taming Trojans to fight around Troy". So they will say, and you will feel new grief as you long for a husband like me to keep you from enslavement. But I would rather be dead and buried than hear your shrieks as you are dragged off.'

So saying, glorious Hector reached out for his child, but the boy screamed and huddled to the breast of his neat nurse, and would not look at his own father, frightened by the bronze and the horse-hair plume, which caught his eye as it nodded terribly over the helmet. His loving father and his royal mother burst out laughing. Glorious Hector put off his shining helmet and laid it on the ground, then took his son and kissed him and rocked him in his arms, and said a prayer to Zeus and the other gods: 'Zeus and you other gods, grant that the Trojans shall look up to this boy as they do to me, and that his strength shall be as mine, and that he shall rule Troy with confidence; and may they say of him on his return from the war, "This one far surpasses his father"; and may he bring back the spoils stained with the blood of the enemy he has killed, and his mother be proud of him.'

With these words he gave his child into his wife's arms, and she took him to her fragrant breast, laughing through tears. Her husband noticed this, and was sorry for her, and patted her and said 'Darling, for my sake don't take this too badly; for no one will send me to Death against my fate. But of this I am sure, that no man, whether he runs away or stands fast, can escape what is fated for him at the moment when he is born into the world.'

In circumstances like this a little society's chance of survival was related directly to the excellence of its menfolk at fighting. If the men were weaklings or cowards, slavery or annihilation awaited them and their dependents just round the corner. The most important quality a man could possess, on which everything else hung, was military prowess. Those who had it, and were successful in preserving their community from danger, had 'virtue', *areté*. 'Best' (*aristos*) meant 'best at fighting'. They were the admired, nobles (*nobiles* – 'distinguished' or 'remarkable' in Latin). Their opposites, the ineffectual, the cowards, the ignoble (or 'undistinguished' – most of us, in fact), were all described by one and the same word, *kakos*, also translated as 'bad'.

The community rewarded the valour of its warrior nobility by paying it 'honour', *timé*, the word also for 'assessment', 'value', or 'price'. This honour consisted in prestige and special material comforts. In their turn, the nobles felt an obligation to display their 'virtue' in valorous deeds when required. Sarpedon, the Lycian ally of Troy in the *Iliad*, when exhorting his fellow-captain Glaucus not to flinch reminds him of this.

Glaucus, why are you and I honoured above all others in Lycia with the highest places at table and the best meat and full cups? Why do all regard us as if we were gods, and allot to us especially a great estate of rich tilth and ploughland by the banks of the Xanthus? It is so that we should now stand in the forefront of the Lycians and face searing battle; and so that the Lycian warriors may say 'Certainly our leaders are not inglorious, who rule in Lycia and eat fine meat and drink choice wine: they deserve it, for their valour too is exceptional, as they fight in the forefront of the Lycian army'.

This honour, this due paid to the champions by their inferiors, was respected by the champion's equals too. By this respect a noble showed his recognition of a fellow-noble, and to flout it was a terrible insult, a slur upon one's manhood.

The heroes' desire to receive honour, their prickly concern for prestige, was almost obsessional. When Agamemnon spitefully robbed him of his prize of war, the girl Briseis, Achilles was so angry that he was ready to endanger the success of the whole Greek expedition, slanging his commander-in-chief before the entire army.

You sot, with the eyes of a dog and the heart of a doe! Have you ever dared to arm with the rest for combat, or take up battle-stations with the Achaean champions? No, for that might be the death of you. You can get far safer spoils from your own side, confiscating the prizes of those who disagree with you. You parasite on your people – who must be nobodies, or this would be your last affront. But I tell you this, Agamemnon, and will seal it with a great oath: by this staff I hold, which will never sprout leaves again, since it was lopped on the mountain-side and stripped of its bark and buds, and now the sons of the Achaeans hold it as they give judgments to safeguard God's laws – it will be a great oath, I tell you: – soon the sons of the Achaeans, each and every one of them, will miss Achilles sorely, when Hector is killing them mercilessly like flies, and you will be able to do nothing for them, however much you want to. Then you will eat your heart out with regret that you showed no respect for the bravest of the Greeks.

If *thymos* moved Homeric man as a living creature, concern for prestige, love of *timé*, moved him as member of society; the former might be called a biological urge, the latter a political one.

The word to describe this thirst for prestige, *philotimia*, was coined by the Greeks of classical times, and had for them very often a bad connotation: an excessive love of prestige. It stands for a social and personal motive of such importance that it will be convenient to wring from it a new English adjective, *philotimous*. The form of our refined modern society differs in many ways from the society depicted in the Homeric poems, but it is still fundamentally *philotimous*.

The motto of the philotimous Homeric hero was 'always to be best and to excel others'. Such an aim engendered, as it was engendered by, an energetic individualism. This is thrown into high relief when we (to our surprise) come upon an example of the opposite, an *aphilotimous* society.

In 1961 the small volcanic island of Tristan da Cunha, in the south Atlantic, erupted, and poisoned the atmosphere. The whole community, which had been established on the island for only a century and a half, and was so tiny and self-sufficient that for five-sixths of its life it had not felt the need to use money, was transported, riddled with toothrot and worms, to Britain. Here, well-meant attempts were made to introduce them to the blessings of a land they had not been promised, to dazzle them with the prizes of mammon. The old were taught new jobs, the young new values. Results were disappointing. I quote a psychologist, who trained a battery of tests on, and closely observed the behaviour of, forty Tristanian children.

We found that life in this community results in some lack of personal initiative, very limited competitiveness, self-acceptance, and in the case of the children, freedom from anxiety, a strong sense of belonging together distinct from 'the outsiders', and a certain fatalism or passivity.

All the children were slow in the basic school subjects; and time produced little change in their personalities. 'A few children, perhaps, were showing rather more interest in their new environment, while passivity decreased and aggression increased.'

This was not the soil in which the growth of *philotimia* could be expected. The Tristanians did not live in constant fear of their neighbours, like the Homeric societies. Perhaps the mysterious 'self-acceptance' would be better described as a lack of self-awareness, of which the strong group feeling was the obverse: the group rather than the individual was the 'conceptual unit'.

The mode of primitive thinking tends to be concrete; nouns stand for palpable things, rather than for abstractions. So, where we might say that a knock on a man's head 'impaired his critical faculties', Homer would say that it 'disturbed his lungs (*phrenes*)'. So too that by virtue of which noblemen were noble, their bravery, or *areté*, was a *thing*, which was revealed or displayed primarily by acts of prowess in battle, but also, more peaceably, by prowess in athletics, the training for the battlefield. A son received his *areté* from his father by birth; it was an heirloom from the founder of the family, who was, in most if not all noble families, a god; for how else to account for the fact that some families had this thing, and the prestige that went with it, while others did not, unless the former were some uncommon seed?

So, to prove their possession of this *areté*, the heroes, before single combat, would boast of their own family and inquire of their foe's, as the Greek Diomedes inquired of Glaucus, and received in reply another Homeric amalgam of old and new, of primitive and wistful.

Impetuous son of Tydeus, why ask whence a man is sprung? Whence do the leaves of the trees spring? Men are no different from them. Just as with the leaves, some flutter to the ground in the wind, but the teeming forest is bringing more to bud, and in the springtime these succeed to those others, so one generation of men waxes as another fades.

But in spite of his observation that men are as indistinguishable from each other by birth as are the leaves of the wood, Glaucus still goes on to give his own noble genealogy.

And as Homer's heroes claimed descent from a god, so noble families in classical Greece would claim descent from a hero; thus asserting their own *semi*-divinity, at least.

So the idea of goodness, or virtue (which for us today has a pre-eminently gentle flavour) was born – in the west, at least – in the province of war, when the warrior discharges a socially useful function which he is best fitted to perform. The word for 'virtue' (or 'excellence'), *areté*, and the word for 'best', *aristos*, are etymologically related; and they may both be related to a verb meaning 'to fit'.

The important point is that goodness at this stage is *functional*: it means 'being good at' something – doing something one is fitted to do. We meet it first applied to the basic need to fight for survival. But we should expect to find it used in other fields as well. The warrior's proper function is to display his bravery in battle; but what is the *areté* of other things, a horse, for instance – or a woman? It will be that which one can do especially well (a horse's *areté* is speed), or what social custom particularly expects of one (a woman's *areté* is to be a faithful wife and a good housekeeper).

So originally society confers status on those who perform a role which is useful to it; and the more useful the role – the more necessary its successful performance to the continuance of the society – the greater the status it earns. A patriarchal society owes a double debt to the father at its head, for he is the source both of its being and its continuance. He is a sort of god to his people, as Sarpedon reminded Glaucus. Zeus himself is father not only of the divine family on Olympus, but of men as well; he is regularly called by Homer, in a formulaic phrase, 'the father of gods and men'. And the status which his household confers on him, the father, reflects back on them. If they lose him, they lose that status also. When Andromache heard that Achilles, returned to the battle, had slain her husband, she lamented for their son that now, even if he escaped death at the hands of the Greeks, he would be friendless.

On the day that a boy loses his father he loses the friendship of his playmates too. He has no confidence for anything, his cheeks are tearstained, and in his need he goes back to those who had been his father's comrades, plucking one by the coat, another by the tunic; and they are sorry for him, and give him a sip from a cup – enough to wet his lips, but not his palate. Then a boy who still has his parents pushes him out, saying 'Go away, *your* father is not at dinner here'.

Even a slave gains status from the part he plays in this little society; the day of enslavement takes away 'half his *areté*', not all of it. When the ghost of Achilles told Odysseus in the underworld that the lowest place among the living is preferable to the highest among the dead, it was not the slave who exemplified for him the most miserable lot on earth, but the unattached man who hires out his labour.

Do not try to play down death to me, Odysseus. I would rather be alive on earth, a servant in the pay of a man who had nothing to pay me with, than king of all the dead.

When we are told that on the day of his enslavement a man 'loses half his *areté*', it really means that he loses *timé*, prestige rather than *areté*, virtue. (This is an ambivalent usage of great importance, which we shall meet again shortly.) The role of the slave carries little prestige, but it carries some. He can feel some self-esteem, because society feels some esteem for him. He is not like Achilles's hired man, or the orphan Astyanax, or beggars, who are outside the scheme of values altogether, worse than failures – they are 'unpersons'.

The outsider (like the failure) becomes dispirited; his *thymos* weakens, he suffers from *athymia*. On the contrary, the successful performance of a part which society has implicitly assigned to one is a tonic for the spirits, one's *thymos* is increased, one is a state of *euthymia*, cheerful and energetic: one feels to be 'someone'. It is in this sense that the group is more 'real' than any individual member of it. This is why exile was such a fearful punishment; to be driven from one's group and to be without a role led to terrible *athymia*. Groups nowadays too know how to use ostracism to devastating effect as a way of disciplining recalcitrant members.

When I talk about 'playing roles' and 'acting parts' I am using metaphors and must be careful. Until the Cynics in late classical times, the Greeks themselves did not apply this metaphor to their social behaviour (the Greek for 'actor' was *hypokrites,* 'hypocrite', without a pejorative sense). And it may be objected that the metaphor appears to put the cart before the horse, the role before the actor.

But it is precisely this which makes the metaphor a fruitful one when considering the emergence of the idea of persons and personality. Even if this particular metaphor did not occur to the classical Greeks, it occurred later to the Romans, for the Latin word *persona* means 'an actor's mask'. Each mask had a set expression, stern or mild, grave or gay; and depicted a set character, king or princess, old man or youth, messenger or slave. The spectators of course knew that beneath the mask was an actor, and that the same actor might be beneath different masks at different times. This suggested an inference about real life: that behind an individual's changing moods and expressions, and his different activities as a member of society, there was a continuing entity. And this entity was given the name 'person' from the only means it had of manifesting itself to others. But is it a metaphor, or is it not? In the theatre of life players and audience are indistinguishable; or rather, the spectators of one drama are the actors in another, and these dramas are intermixed and run concurrently. 'All the world's a stage, and all the men and women merely players': when men and women *come to see themselves* as players they have in fact taken a great step in their own individuation – 'persons' are being born. Though it was classical Greece that saw the flowering of ancient drama, it was Rome, the cultural slave of Greece and not noteworthy for its playwrights, that helped the *person* to birth. But this is to run far ahead; beyond the child's birth, almost to its christening. We are still studying its gestation, though we have now had a sight of its parents, *thymos* and *philotimia*: the general biological drive for survival joined to the particularising drive for social status.

In course of time, as life became more settled, the occasions that called for warlike valour became less frequent, and the opportunities dwindled for the nobles to display that *areté* which was their birthright. But it might still be needed at any moment, and even though it might be in cold storage, as it were, the honour, *timé*, due to it was still paid, in the form of privileges, to the families in which it was thought to dwell.

It was easy to see the continued rendering of this honour as manifest evidence that the virtue, *areté*, to which it was owed was still there. The son may in fact have been much inferior to his father, but the reassurance of his own virtue which the son received at the same time with these honours would work for the survival of the aristocratic system which produced them, quite as much as the physical comforts they brought. Only the nobles could change the system, and it no more occurred to them to do so (why should it?) than it occurred to the nonentities – the men of no family and no virtue – who comprised the mass of society. Throughout the Homeric epics only one such, Thersites ('Bigmouth'), stood forth to attack the greed and selfishness of the princes. The Achaean host, of whose resentments he might seem to us to be the mouthpiece, in fact warmly applauded the beating he received from Odysseus in return.

It is not surprising then that the pursuit of virtue's *reward* (*timé*), – *philotimia*, 'desire for status', – came to replace the pursuit of virtue itself. The reception of honour seemed to guarantee that the recipient possessed virtue, rather than the other way about. The shadow replaced the substance, the image the reality.

By the time the Homeric poems were being committed to writing in the approximate form in which we have them (about 750-650 BC), that older aristocratic society whose values they depict was beginning to change. Though the Greek world was to be riddled with wars and bloody quarrels for half a millennium more, and peace was to be regarded until the fourth century as an 'absence of war' rather than as normal, yet already it was communicating more easily within itself and with the outside. Trade gets scant mention in the embattled *Iliad*, but Phoenician merchant adventurers feature in the *Odyssey*, and they must have been familiar enough to the poet's public. Neither poem betrays any knowledge of coined money, but the spread of this invention was at hand, assisting a new mobility of wealth which was to be reflected in an unprecedented mobility in the elements of society.

The wealth of the old warrior aristocracy, that manifest evaluation of their virtue, that *timé* which symbolised their *areté*, was basically the static wealth of land and the products of land, crops and cattle. Now, with the spread of comparative peace and trade, two things were happening: the valour of the individual was less needed by society, and the wealth which stood for latent valour, or virtue, was becoming more widely accessible. We have remarkable evidence for the beginning of this process in the poem called *Works and Days*, of the early seventh century B.C. Though it uses the verse and language of epic, its tone is far removed from the aristocratic tone of Homer. In fact its author, Hesiod, is almost an embodiment of the ill-bred Thersites, in his continual railing at the 'corrupt princelings' whose venal verdict had cheated him of his due inheritance.

The poet was a crusty old farmer, whose father had left Asia Minor for the Greek mainland and settled in the village of Ascra, on the edge of the fertile Boeotian plain at the foot of Mount Helicon. Helicon was the home of the Muses, and Hesiod says he once met them there. If he reports them correctly, they were blunt-spoken ladies, who inspired Hesiod with their own forthrightness.

The burden of the *Works and Days* is one of almost unrelieved woe. Land and sea are full of evils; times go from bad to worse, corruption is rife, there is no justice anywhere; Ascra in particular is no place to live, 'harsh in winter, unbearable in summer, wretched at any time'. There is only one thing to do: work hard, and so accumulate wealth. 'Work is no shame, but idleness is. If you work, the idle will soon be envying your wealth; and wealth brings with it virtue (*areté*) and esteem.'

Again: 'Worthlessness is the prize of the masses; the way to it is smooth, and the journey short. But the immortal gods have stationed Sweat to guard Virtue (*areté*): steep and long is the path to her, and rough at first; yet when you have reached the heights, hard as she was to win she is easy to hold.' That is, *areté* (the virtue of effort, which is hard) leads to riches, which enable you to enjoy without further effort the reputation for *areté*.

These passages bring out the widening sense of the word *areté*, to cover both the thing itself and its symbol; the reality and the image.

The Hesiodic idea of 'virtue' was a direct challenge to the aristocratic 'virtue' of Homer, which was a thing confined to certain families and handed down by birth. Hesiod asserts that any ordinary man can acquire it, if he is prepared to toil. Even so, the newly-arising aristocracy of wealth was not immune to the glamour of the old aristocracy of birth, and was eager enough to insure the virtue it had won, and to secure it by marriage with the older families; which were themselves not above compounding to this extent with the degeneracy of the times, as one sixth-century aristocrat complained.

We look for breeding in our cattle, and want to make our purchases out of good stock. Yet a nobleman thinks nothing of marrying the common daughter of a commoner, if only she brings him wealth. Again, if a man has wealth but no worth, a woman will not refuse him, but prefers a husband with riches to one with birth. It is in money that they all see value (*timé*), and hence the precious is united with the base, the base with the precious. Wealth has stirred lineage in the melting-pot.

2

The Birth of the Anti-Hero

The tension between the old aristocrats, whose claims to *areté* were based on birth, and the new timocrats, men of no family but measuring their worth by the standard of material wealth, was to work itself out over the next couple of centuries throughout the Greek world in the setting of the city-state (*polis*).

This was a small, self-contained and independent community, in which, when fully developed, political power was wielded, not by a limited class of nobles, but by the whole body of citizens (*politai*) – which, however, was far from comprising the whole population, as women, slaves and foreign residents were excluded from it.

Essentially, the city-state was based not on family or tribal relationships but on locality. It implied a settled community, clustered about a customary centre of congregation which was the kernel of a town. Perhaps the germ of it was the Mycenaean fortress-palaces, round which the ruler's dependents huddled for protection, like cottagers round a baronial castle. Anyway, the city-state was the vessel through which the values of an earlier, aristocratic society, suspended in literary form in Homer the educator of Greece, were conveyed to a wider agglomerate, to be soaked up and later again precipitated.

All its members were subject to the rule of law, *nomos* – a word which first had the sense of 'custom' rather than what we understand as 'law'. Early law was codified custom, written down and replacing the verbal interpretation of unwritten custom which the nobles had pronounced (as a sort of *common law*) when they held court in earlier days. Such jurisdiction was open to abuse, as Hesiod had grumbled; codification meant that, ideally at least, all were 'equal before the law'. But this was not the case continually in the city-state, which preserved a reminder of its origin in a perpetual antagonism between the old noble families and their adherents, the Few (*hoi oligoi*, the oligarchs), and the Many, the body of the citizens (*hoi polloi*).

But a most important effect of the evolving city-state was that, for more individuals, it multiplied the roles they could play in the community. The democratic city-state offered more actors more parts, and more changes of part. In addition to the set roles demanded of a man as a member of his clan, or tribe, or village, he might now, *for limited periods*, be mayor, or general, or judge, or councillor; any citizen might now assume temporarily roles which had once been the unquestioned birthright of certain families. The skein of functions once performed by the nobleman, for the performance of which he had been paid his *timé*, his meed of honour, was fragmented and distributed among the people as offices; and the word *timé* acquired a new sense, of 'office'. The word denoting the reward for the proper function of a role was extended to mean the mere playing of the role, whether well or badly being immaterial.

The easing of communications between peoples which accompanied the spread of commerce and colonisation was working by another path towards the same end, the idea of personal individuation. Psychologists have noted that frequent changes of environment enhance the sense of 'selfhood', and it is perhaps no wonder that the much-travelled Odysseus, 'who saw the cities of many men and came to know their outlooks', was the most versatile of the heroes.

A similar result may be produced by the presence of strangers in a community. If this occurs frequently enough, the fact that other, different, cultures exist will be borne in on the hosts. But if it is rare, it may issue merely in attempts to integrate the stranger into the community on customary lines, like those Australian aborigines mentioned by Ralph Linton, who would try to find a point of contact in the intruder's genealogy with a genealogy in their own tribe. If they discovered such a point of contact, they knew how to treat him, and could 'assign him a series of statuses which immediately fit[ted] him into the social body'. But if they failed in their search, they could think of nothing else to do but kill him. This process is not unlike the way in which we ourselves tend to categorise strangers, to slot them into ready-made classifications – as 'public-school', 'socialist', 'Roman Catholic', for example – in order to know what face we should present to them, and to assess their probable reactions. The stages of 'getting to know' someone are a refinement of this process, culminating – in what? In the realisation that he is ultimately an *unclassifiable individual*? Or that he is only the nodal point of very many classifications? If the latter, he is a puppet (a slave of the *philotimous* system, perhaps!), and ultimately manageable by the social engineer; if the former, he is essentially a free man.

The Homeric heroes had a more refined solution than that of Linton's aborigines to the problem of how to deal with a stranger. If you entertain such a one, a bond of 'guest-friendship' is formed between you and him – the Greek word for 'stranger', 'host' and 'guest' was the same, *xenos* – which ensures that he will give you similar treatment if you are ever in his country; and furthermore this new relationship is one which is inherited by your respective families. This idea became even more civilised later, with the formalisation of the *proxenos* (a sort of proconsul), who was designated in one city to be the *xenos* of any visitor from a certain other city.

The first stage on the road to selfhood from the reservoir of consciousness is a dual process. On the one hand there is a distinction, increasingly felt, between subject and object, perceiver and percept. On the other, there comes an awareness of an entity continuing constant at the centre of the changing environment and activity: it is the same 'I' which works, eats, plays, loves.

This distinction is both reflected and promoted in the development of language, but remains ambiguous – men speak of the world as if it were both inside and outside them – until the evolution of mathematics, which is at once most objective and most abstract, most remote from 'the world' (there can be no 'science of individuals', *de particularibus philosophia esse non poterit*).

Immediately on top of this 'biological selfhood' accrues 'social selfhood', wherein the society into which the individual is born corresponds to the environmental world of the 'biological self', and the varying roles which he learns to play in his society correspond to the various activities – eating, working, and so on – which emphasise the continuity of the 'biological self'. The social 'person' is an extrapolation from his varying *personae*, the continuing entity behind the different masks of his changing roles.

Men partake of biological and social selfhood insofar as they are biological organisms living in societies. In Greece a third self, channelled and moulded between the two faces of *thymos* and *philotimia*, was manifested, and superimposed on these two others. I call it the 'heroic self', as Homer's heroes are its exemplars. Through the vehicle of the city-state and the medium of the Homeric poems, which became the primary textbooks of Greek education, this prototype was to spread and multiply – every citizen was an embryonic hero or king – until it appeared to be the essence of manliness, or 'being human'.

I do not mean to suggest that every Attic farmer tending his olives actually thought of himself as an Achilles, but that the mainspring of his actions as a member of society was that of Achilles and the rest of the heroes: concern for his evaluation by others, his *timé*. And the fundamental *timé* of an Attic farmer in classical Greece of the fifth century BC lay in his possession of citizen rights, the loss of which was technically called *atimia*, 'the loss of *timé*'. (The holding of magisterial offices, on the other hand, conferred additional *timé*.)

This implies a philotimous basis assumed for social action, at least in Athens (which is indeed our main example, of necessity). I have said that *philotimia* often had a bad sense; yet in the first appearance of the word known to us this is not so: a poet warns against 'excessive *philotimia*' in the state. This of course implies that there can be moderate *philotimia*, which presumably is at least not injurious to the social body. And in a prologue to a lost play of Euripides we are told that Odysseus (very much a 'man of the world' for this tragedian) ruminated whether he, who had the reputation of being the most sagacious of men, was not in fact the most foolish: for though he could if he wished live a life of inaction free from worries, he had chosen the perilous life of a man of affairs. He found the cause of this choice in that *philotimia* of men of talent and 'family', who undertake the heaviest burdens for the sake of reputation; for 'there is nothing in nature as proud as Man'. Through the mouth of the old hero, Euripides is here putting the point of view of his own ambitious contemporaries of the latter part of the fifth century, eager to make their mark in politics, who would share the contempt of the Athenian statesman Pericles for inaction, whether in a citizen or his city. By now the city was the field wherein the game of status-seeking, *philotimia*, was played between citizens, and it was also the *persona* presented by the citizen-body to the world outside, through which the respect, *timé*, felt by foreigners was mediated to the individual citizen, who was elated by his state's successes and was downcast by its failures.

The ambivalent attitude of Aristotle, in the following century, to *philotimia* is interesting. An important part of Aristotle's moral theory is that virtue is not the opposite of vice, but is a mean between vices. Put another way: particular vices are an excess or a defect of a particular virtue; for example, courage is the virtue, an excess of which is the vice of foolhardiness, and a defect of which is the vice of cowardice. To him *philotimia* is a vice, because it is an excess of something; but he admits that it is sometimes praised, and this, he says, is because the virtue of which it is an excess has not been given a name (and therefore gets confused with it). He shrewdly remarks that most people, through *philotimia*, want to be courted rather than to pay court, and that men want the *timé* of the respectable and the judicious, because this reassures them in their own good opinion of themselves.

Vicious *philotimia* is an ambitious desire to improve one's status; virtuous *philotimia* is a concern to preserve the status one already has, without necessarily implying any concern to improve it. It therefore assumes without question the rightness of the *status quo*, a fundamental assumption of aristocracies (and indeed, of democracies too): Achilles in the *Iliad* resented the diminution of his *timé* by Agamemnon, but showed no wish to supplant his commander-in-chief. Nothing is more indicative of the essentially aristocratic nature of Greek society (in Athens, the mother of democracy) than the fact that Aristotle found no name for the virtuous *philotimia*: as a social motive it was so inbuilt that no one had noticed it until he did!

This growing self-awareness produced, in the sixth century

BC, an event of the first importance: the beginning of philosophy. Yet philosophy did not start with speculation about man himself, as one might have expected, but about man's universe. Until then natural events and natural objects had been explained by myth: the earth and the sky, day and night, stars and sea and rivers, the gods as well, were members of a great cosmic family, branches of a family tree sharing a common ancestry, born of parents and themselves having offspring. These different entities had come into being, each as it is, each with its own province and its own business (one would not sow the sea with crops, nor would one fish in the earthy fields). They were *persons*, each with its role.

Now, as the notion was forming (though as yet covert), of a single continuous 'self' behind the changing masks of the social man, men began to think of the physical world in a similar way; to want to see a single substance as underlying the multiple variations of natural phenomena. ('Substance' is a philosophical abstraction and an anachronism when used in the context of the sixth century BC, but there lay the beginning of the concept.) These variations were not to be thought of as brought about by a multitude of different agents, as myth had it, but as modifications of one of their number. The first developed theory of which we have any extensive knowledge was the ingenious one that all things are vapour in one of its guises, vapour rarefied or densified to a greater or lesser degree; an idea suggested no doubt by observing vapour condensing into water, congealing into ice, or evanescing into air. And air, or breath, can be hot or cold, so might not the extremes of these processes be the tenuous heat of fire and the cold solidity of earth?

In this way the unity of all things came to be seen in a new light: they are not merely a unity in the sense that they are all members of one family (as we have seen, the family or 'house', rather than the individual member of it, would be the conceptual unit for the earlier Greeks), but they are a physical unity in the sense that they are all made of the same stuff or substance. (The word 'physical' is derived from the noun *physis* (in Latin, *natura*), which comprised both the sense of the process of *coming-to-be* or growing, and the sense of *being*, that which comes-to-be or grows; that is, a particular 'natural' object, or more generally the stuff of which objects are made, which gives them their particular character, their 'nature'.)

In another way also speculation about the make-up of the world he lived in reflected man's increasing sense of individuation: in the theory of atomism which emerged in the fifth century BC, with the postulate of the physical *individual* – quite literally – the *uncleavable* atom (*atomos*, 'unsplittable'). Myriads of these, all alike in having no qualities beyond shape, size and indivisibility, produce the manifold diversity of nature by clustering in different arrangements to form different objects.

Yet in the city-state, for all its complexity, the idea of 'selfhood', though emerging, was still only latent. Indeed, Greek and Latin were never to evolve a noun meaning 'the self'. The city was still greater than its citizens, as the family had been greater than its members (if they were not heroes), and it was a bold suggestion of the unorthodox Euripides that 'the state was composed of men'. It was the state that mourned the loss of those killed in war, and it was for the state's glory that they died; the private grief was hardly noticed.

Nevertheless, membership of the city-state was producing moral dilemmas, the formulation of which helped to point up as independent moral agents those who had to try to resolve them. Art, in the hands of the great Athenian tragedians of the fifth century, led the process by focusing men's attention on these problems, isolating and posing them rather than answering them.

The *Antigone* of Sophocles presented one such dilemma, clothed in the garb of the bygone heroic age: the clash of familial piety and religious duty with the interests of the state. To assert his claim to rule his native city of Thebes, Polyneices had led an army against it and his brother Eteocles, who had usurped the throne. During the repulse of the onslaught the brothers met in combat, and both fell. Their uncle Creon, who saw himself now as the rightful inheritor of the supreme power, in order to disgrace and punish the man who had attacked his own fatherland, forbade the rites of burial to the corpse of Polyneices (to deny rest to his soul). Antigone, the sister of the royal brothers, disobeyed the order. For this Creon condemned her to death, so starting a train of events which ended in the deaths of his own son and wife – in effect, the cutting off of his family.

Both the protagonists in the play are obstinate in their convictions. Creon, harsh and overbearing, expresses the attitude which the state must adopt in matters touching its very existence. On his entry he declares his principles of government: the interests of the city come first, before any calls of friendship or kinship, and must be promoted fearlessly in word and deed.

> A governor who, in his guidance of his city, gives advice that is not the best, checking his tongue because he is the prisoner of some fear, such a one is to me the worst of men; while one who values his friend above his own country, him I do not reckon as a man at all.

Creon sees himself, the head of the state, as the sole interpreter and executor of the state's good; any opposition to, any questioning of, his word is insubordination, the ruin of cities. For dramatic purposes, he *is* the state.

> Whomsoever the state has set over it, he must be obeyed in small things and in great, be his ordinances fair or unfair. There is no greater evil than anarchy, for anarchy destroys states, razes homes, breaks ranks and routs armies.

Antigone, when caught in her act of disobedience and charged with it before Creon, is proud to have obeyed a law which she fearlessly asserts to be greater than the king's.

> This prohibition was not from Zeus. Such an order never had the sanction of Justice, who dwells with the gods of the dead; nor did I think that your proclamation could outweigh the unshakeable and unwritten laws of the gods, and authorise a mortal to transgress them. God's laws are not things of a day, but everlasting, and none can name a day when they were born. The fear of some man's whim could never drive me to incur the penalty of breaking these, a penalty which the gods would exact. I shall die, of course I shall, your proclamation notwithstanding. If I die before my time, it will be for me an escape from misery and a blessing – no pain. If I had suffered the corpse of my brother to lie unburied, that would have been pain for me; but this is not.

Antigone did die for her convictions. But it would be a mistake to see her as a martyr in the cause of individual freedom against the tyranny of the state. Though the clash is represented by Sophocles as between divine and human law, the moral standard which both champions assume, that which provides their motivation, is one and the same: it is the standard of the philotimous man, the seeker after the approval of others. The question at issue in the play is, whose approval is to be sought? Antigone prefers that of the gods and her dead kinsmen. If she is killed for burying her brother, if she is condemned for 'the crime of piety', she will nevertheless dwell in the world below in friendship with him and with her parents – and we shall have to please the dead, she says drily, for a longer time than we shall have to please the living.

So Antigone's code is still the philotimous code: to do what earns the approval of your friends, those who have like interests with you, and to harm your enemies – those whose interests clash with the interests of your group, and so with your interests. It is the code professed by Creon himself in his dispute with his son Haemon about Antigone (whom Haemon loves). A father, Creon says, prays to bring up sons obedient to his will, in order that the friends he honours they may honour too, and the enemies who injure him they may repay with harm.

As I have said, when the Greeks began to turn from myth to philosophy they first focused their attention, not on themselves, but on their environment; not on man but on nature, to beg the question in another way. Because of this, the Ionian Greeks of the sixth century BC have been called 'the first scientists'. So long as it is realised that they had almost nothing of modern scientific method, the title is not altogether undeserved; but it is a misnomer when it is used to discredit as 'unscientific' those who followed them in the fifth century, for whom man occupied the centre of the stage.

The changed viewpoint is epitomised by a chorus in that same *Antigone*, which was produced in 442 BC. Two centuries before, the pessimistic Hesiod had seen a man's struggle with his stubborn and hostile environment as the way the man might demonstrate his *areté*, and, if victorious, win wealth which would confer upon him the *timé* of his fellows. This was the most that could be hoped for, that the odd farmer here and there might wring enrichment from the grudging elements. But the Sophoclean chorus sees Man (not just some men) as the victor over Nature.

There are some strange things, but nothing stranger than man. He thrusts through the spume veils of the stormy sea, riding its abyssal surge; and from the supreme goddess, the unwearying, imperishable Earth herself, he exacts tribute, scarifying her perennially with the plough, as it cuts the zigzag furrows by the labour of the equine breed. Cheating the bobbing minds of the birds, and the tribes of beasts, and the brood of the salt sea, he ensnares them in the toils of woven nets, does cunning man. Through devices he masters the wild denizens of the mountain, and yokes to his service horses and tireless bulls.

He has taught himself speech, and thoughts restless as the wind, has learnt the law-abiding disposition societies need, and how to shun the bitter shafts of storm and frost from the bare sky. He is all-resourceful; he faces no eventuality without the wit to meet it. He has planned escape from invincible diseases, and will all but circumvent Death.

Man has risen above the beasts by his twin abilities of speech and reason, which are also the bases of his ability to form peaceful associations with his fellow-men, his capacity for *civilisation*. He is on the way to conquering Nature, and is preparing to challenge God. Such a challenge was abhorrent to Sophocles, but not to his elder contemporary Aeschylus, whose startling play *Prometheus in Chains* must have been produced (if it really is his) fifteen years before *Antigone*. In this play man's mastery of his environment is represented as an offence against a jealous and tyrannical God, who punishes it by a sort of crucifixion of the human spirit, symbolised by Prometheus. (Prometheus, though divine to the playwright and his audience, was not one of the family of Zeus on Olympus but the personification of an abstraction, as is shown by his name, which may be rendered as 'Foresight'.)

The play opens on the scene of Prometheus's punishment – a bleak rock in an arctic desert, on which he is to be spread-eagled. Enter the execution party, with the condemned guarded by Zeus's unattractive handmaidens, Power and Force, and the craftsman god Hephaestus to execute reluctantly his father's sentence on another god, for whom he shows open sympathy – although Prometheus is guilty of the theft, on man's behalf, of Hephaestus's own fire, the wherewithal of technological advance.

Proceedings are directed by Power, high-pitched and almost hysterical. 'Why so slow? Fetter his wrists, hammer, peg him to the rock . . . Tighter yet, or he'll slip out somehow . . . Don't forget the body-irons . . . Now ring his legs firmly . . . This will teach him that he cannot outsmart Zeus . . . Now nail him through the chest . . . No pity, or you may find yourself in a like fix . . . There now, let us see if our planner can plan his way out of that.'

Later, Prometheus confesses his sin of *philanthropy* to the chorus. Before him men 'had eyes that saw not, ears that heard not, but they drifted their long life through in aimless muddle, like dream-shapes. They knew no carpentry, or the warmth of brick-woven houses, but lived deep in the sunless crannies of caves, no different from ants. They had no way to mark the season of the onset of winter's storms, or of the spring flowers, or of the fruits of summer, but all they did they did unknowingly, till I taught them how to make a calendar from the risings and settings of the stars, a difficult lesson.'

Yes, and it was I who taught them the most ingenious trick of all, number, and the flexible alphabet, a universal monument, the servant-girl who has mothered the Muses. I was the first to harness the power of beasts to relieve men of their hardest labours; and none other invented sailing-ships, to wing men far and wide over the seas.

All this, and other attainments too – the conquest of disease, the forecasting of the future – in fact all sciences must be credited to Prometheus, who confesses that, for all the good he has done others, himself he cannot save from his present pains.

The chorus advises him to think of himself first, and then, surely, he will find freedom from his fetters and be God's equal. (At the end of the play a different solution is foreshadowed: Prometheus, who is divine and so cannot die, will be released from his torture when he can find some other immortal who will be willing to renounce his immortality and descend into the House of Death in Prometheus's place.)

The picture of man as potentially the master of his circumstances and independent of the divine power was completed and promoted by the so-called sophists, the most famous of whom, from the middle to the end of the fifth century, travelled about Greece imparting their teaching to any who were prepared to pay them a fee. For a teacher to make a charge for his services was a novelty, a novelty which incurred the disapproval of the austere, but the name 'sophist' did not at first have the connotation of fraud which it later acquired. It merely meant something like 'expert', but the expertise which the sophists professed was a broad one: how to succeed in life.

These itinerant professors did not have their roots in the Greek motherland, but came from the outlying and newer foundations. They were individualists, and it is perhaps no accident that the first of them, Protagoras, came from the same city as Democritus, the traditional father of the atomic theory, and was supposed to have been his associate.

Protagoras was the author of a relativistic theory of knowledge: that our statements about our world are not (as they appear to be) about objects outside us, but about our perceptions of those objects, and therefore still true even if another's statement contradicts them. If John says the bath is hot but Jane says it is cool they are only apparently contradicting each other, for they are not really talking about the same thing: John is talking about a relationship, John-with-bath, and Jane is talking about a different relationship, Jane-with-bath. This theory is clearly connected with the most famous of Protagoras's sayings that have been preserved, that 'the man is the measure of all things'; that is, the observer is the sole arbiter of his own observations. Protagoras's remark is commonly rendered as 'man is the measure of all things', whatever that is supposed to mean. But however we take it, the implication of man's self-reliance is still there, and it is not surprising that this sophist's dismissal of theology was peremptory and sardonic: 'The subject is obscure, and life is short.'

This sophistic type of man, this apprentice in the art of

fate-mastery and soul-captaincy, already presented to us in universal terms in the chorus of *Antigone* which I have quoted, and in parabolic terms in the figure of the Aeschylean Prometheus, is given flesh and blood in the person of Ajax, in the play of that name by Sophocles. Here the hero, who had wrestled with Odysseus for the arms of the dead Achilles, has lost, and the mere imagination of his enemies' exultation over his discomfiture maddens him, so that he slaughters a flock of sheep in the delusion that they are his mockers. Returned to his senses, the conviction that this misdirected vengeance will make him an even greater laughing-stock drives him to suicide.

What is of interest here is not the self-importance of Ajax so much as his enormous (really introverted and morbid) pre-occupation with it. What matters to him is what he thinks people are thinking of him, not what they actually are thinking (in fact his chief adversary Odysseus turns out to be surprisingly sympathetic to him). Ajax is the best type of philotimous man, anxious for prestige, but also anxious to have deserved it entirely by his own efforts (*areté*). Though born a man, he had thoughts above his station; and an illustration of this was recalled after his death.

> Even when he first left home for the war, he was shown to be a fool. For then his father sensibly advised him to pray for victory, but only for victory with God's aid. But he returned a vain and reckless answer: 'Father, with God's aid even a nobody could win the mastery. I am determined to snatch glory with or without it.'

The sophists professed to teach men *areté*. It will be recalled that for the aristocratic Homer *areté* was something inborn in certain families, handed down like an heirloom; something which might or might not be *displayed* by its possessor, but which could never be *taught* to one who had not already got it in him. The plebeian Hesiod, on the other hand, held that it could be acquired by anyone, by hard work; for him, *areté* was teachable.

The sophists were on the side of Hesiod in this disagreement; but the *areté* which they, the moderns, claimed to impart was neither military prowess nor rustic industry. What then was it? Plato made his master Socrates put this very question to the arch-sophist Protagoras, in the dialogue called after him, and made Protagoras reply with the following myth or fable.

When the gods had modelled the beasts and man out of clay, and the time was approaching for them to be animated and born into the sunlight, they delegated to two subordinate deities, the brothers Prometheus and Epimetheus ('Foresight' and 'Hindsight'), the task of assigning to the various species their various characteristics. Epimetheus, a busybody with a strong desire to shine, induced his brother to leave to him the actual allocation, and to content himself with merely checking the job when it had been done.

So Epimetheus dealt out his stock of characteristics to each species: horns and claws with which to defend themselves to some, while to the weaker he gave the power to take refuge in the air or in burrows. Against the inclemencies of the seasons he gave them thick skins and fur. And he made some to be vegetarians, others to feed off these; but to ensure that no species was extinguished he arranged for the former to be prolific, and the carnivores the reverse. Unfortunately, when he came to the end of the queue Epimetheus found he had nothing left to bestow upon man; and it was from this plight that Prometheus rescued his brother, by stealing from the gods fire, which equipped man to some extent against his hostile environment.

However, the secrets of technology looked to be insufficient for this purpose, unless men learned also the secret of co-operation; and this Prometheus had not been able to steal, for it was the secret of Zeus himself. Now when it seemed that the human race might be wiped out, Zeus was worried because men are related to the gods (as is shown by the fact that they alone of living creatures have an idea of deity); so he sent his messenger Hermes to them with two gifts from his own store – a sense of shame and a sense of justice. Hermes asked him how he was to share these gifts out: 'In the way the crafts have been shared out, so that a few experts serve many laymen with their knowledge? Or shall I distribute them to all men equally?' Zeus replied that he was to share them among all men equally, 'for societies could not exist, if there were laymen in the art of communal living, as there are laymen in the crafts and sciences. And' he added, 'implant this custom in them from me: that if there should be any without a sense of justice and a shame of wrongdoing, they are to cut him out like a cancer from the body politic.'

This then, is the *areté* which all men have (if they are men and not monsters): the ability to co-operate together in communities, to live politically. It will be seen that this is really a compromise between the Homeric and Hesiodic positions. Instead of a simple opposition between the idea of virtue inborn in a few (though not always displayed), and the idea that virtue can be acquired by all, we have the suggestion that virtue is inborn in everyone, but is elicited by training.

Protagoras does not say in his fable that man is co-operative *by nature*; in fact he rather goes out of his way to distinguish the human gift for co-operation from those 'natural' characteristics – wings or fur or vegetarianism or the rest – dispensed by Epimetheus to the other creatures. Man's capability of forming societies he owes to his relationship with God; it is a divine attribute.

The distinction seems to be based on a feeling that there is a fundamental gap between physiological and psychological qualities. This gap was closing, with the developing concept of 'nature' (*physis*).

A Greek of the fifth century would have been puzzled if you had spoken to him of 'Mother Nature', but would have understood well enough if you said that 'lions have fierce natures', or 'wood has a combustible nature, *physis*'. I have already said that the Greek word comprises the senses of 'being', 'constitution', 'properties', with those of 'coming-to-be', 'origin', 'birth'. The obvious fact that things are like what they come from, that like begets like, led to the assumption that not only would the off-spring of lions be lions and of men, men, but that a particular man would have the same nature, *physis*, as his father (the mother's contribution to her child's constitution was hardly considered at this time, far less understood, by the man-in-the-street).

This was, of course, the basis of the Homeric idea of *areté* being handed down in noble families. It is expressed much later than Homer, by Sophocles in his play *Philoctetes*, but with an interesting development. A scheme to blackmail Philoctetes, devised by Odysseus, is foiled on the point of success when its instrument, Achilles's youthful son Neoptolemus, cannot bring himself to follow it through. 'By this,' cries delighted Philoctetes to him, 'you have shown the stock (*physis*) from which you are sprung: no foxy Sisyphus [Odysseus's father], but one who always had the reputation of a gentleman, Achilles.' The point that 'breeding will out' is made more than once in this play, but Sophocles presents us with a new psychological insight. 'It rankles all the time', says Neoptolemus, 'when one goes against one's nature, and acts out of character.' There is no categorical imperative here that one ought to act according to one's *physis*, nor obviously is there any mechanistic imperative that one *must* necessarily do so; only a statement of fact, that not to do so produces mental discomfort.

The idea of *physis* as universally inborn or innate character or potentiality, as a *general* principle of 'nature', was not precipitated until the fifth century, which discerned in it one of a pair of opposing principles of behavioural causation: *physis* and *nomos* ('custom' or 'law'). The distinction was not apparent to Homer, where the word *physis* appears once and the word *nomos* not at all. Though Homer's Odysseus had 'seen the cities of many men, and came to know their outlooks', it was the Ionian Greeks much later, with their extended knowledge of, and interest in, geography and anthropology, who saw that the variegated ways of the single species, man, are caused by his upbringing in varying traditions or conventions (*nomoi*). This is brought out in a telling little tale by Herodotus.

Darius, after he had got the kingdom [of Persia], called into his presence certain Greeks who were at hand, and asked what he should pay them to eat the bodies of their fathers when they died. To which they answered that there was no sum that would tempt them to do such a thing. He then sent for certain Indians, of the race called Callatians, men who eat their fathers, and asked them, while the Greeks stood by, and knew by the help of an interpreter all that was said, what he should give them to burn their fathers at their decease. The Indians exclaimed in horror, and bade him forbear such language. Such are the ordinances of custom, and Pindar was right, in my judgment, when he said 'Custom is the king o'er all'.

The sophists were individualists, each hawking around his own brand of individualism. There was one freakish but very interesting brand: that of Hippias of Elis, who professed to teach men how to be self-sufficient in an economic sense. The old *polis* community had subsisted as a self-sufficient economic unit; now each one of us can be a *polis* in himself! Anyone who could in fact do this could dispense with society, and would be like Aristotle's God, complete in himself and needing the exertions of no other.

For the attainment of this end, one had merely to know all crafts and all sciences, and be able to practise them. This theory and practice Hippias claimed to be able to impart, and as some earnest of his claim he appeared at the Olympic games dressed entirely in things he had made himself.

But the aim of other sophists was to teach men, not how to detach themselves from society by being able to minister each to his own wants, but how to succeed within society on society's own terms – within the philotimous system, in other words. Though their idea of *areté* was much more sophisticated than that of the Homeric hero, they still accepted as basic the hero's motto, 'always to be best and to excel others'.

But what, in the much more civilised society of the fifth-century city-state, was the equivalent of the physical prowess of the old heroic age? It was to be able to assert one's will, not by deeds (which might disrupt the delicate framework on which the social web was hung), but by words. The sophists' interest fastened on the power of words: how, by means of words alone, you can make other men's wishes coincide with your own (or, at second best, cow their opposition into silence). A new art was being added to the old arts of the carpenter, the potter, the smith – the art of the persuader, the art of oratory.

The power of words, and how to use that power to convince your audience, by appealing to their emotion or their reason – that was the chief art of the sophists. The skills of rhetoric and of dialectic originated mainly with them, no mean achievement. And undeniably these skills could be put to the disinterested service of other people; as one sophist defined it, *areté* consists in furthering law and justice, the interest of the majority. But they could be used by an unscrupulous individual quite differently, to subjugate others to *his* desires; a danger which tempered the warmth with which the sophists were received.

This danger and its implications make the theme of a Platonic dialogue named after the sophist Gorgias, who was credited with the invention of the art of rhetoric. At one point in the dialogue Socrates asks Gorgias what advantage the acquisition of his art brings with it. The master replies that it brings the greatest advantage of all: it makes its possessor a free man, for in whatever company he may be he can ensure that his views will prevail; he will even be able to override experts in the subject under debate, if they are unversed in the art of persuasion. Finally, however, on being subjected to a Socratic inquisition, Gorgias mildly admits that this could lead to grave injustice being done, and that the orator should also be 'a good man'. So, rejoins Socrates, Gorgias's art does not after all bring the greatest advantage, which is to know good from evil.

The great man's complacency is not shared by some of his younger admirers, who are listening with growing impatience, and who think that he has conceded Socrates's point much too readily. One, who rushes to take up the cudgels on Gorgias's behalf, ends by being driven even further, to the admission that to suffer wrong is actually preferable to doing it, and that to escape punishment for one's wrongdoing is the worst fate of all. This paradox stings another, one Callicles, into a contemptuous tirade, which has been portentous in its influence on European history.

You say you are pursuing truth, Socrates, but you are just like a cheap tub-thumper really, confusing what is conventionally good with what is naturally good. But nature (*physis*) and convention (*nomos*) are generally diametrically opposed; so that a man is compelled to contradict himself if he is ashamed to speak out what he really thinks. This is the great trick you use to cheat in arguments, switching the ground of your questions according to whether your opponent bases his answers on convention or on nature. This is what happened just now – for to do wrong is baser by convention, but by nature to be wronged is baser, for in nature there is no distinction between 'baser' and 'worse'. Anyway, what sort of a man, I ask you, would put up with being wronged? No one but a mere slave, who would be better dead than alive, since he can't protect himself or those he cares about from harm and insults. In my opinion conventions and laws are framed by the weaklings – which is to say, the majority of mankind. So they make laws and apportion praise and blame as their own interests dictate, from fear of the stronger . . . This is why it is conventionally considered unjust and disgraceful to try to get more than the rest; yet I think that nature itself shows that the lion's share should go to the better and more able. You can find universal proof of this, not only among animals, but in human societies.

I could give thousands of examples. What right did Xerxes have to march against Greece, or his father Darius against the Scythians? The right that nature gave them, that's all – I dare call it nature's own 'convention', though certainly it is not ours. *We* catch our lions when they are cubs, the best and strongest of our number, and tame them into slaves by mazing them with incantations to the effect that we must all be equal, and that this equality is a fine and just thing. But let one of sufficient spirit (*physis*) shake all this off, break his tether and make for freedom, and he will trample on all our runes and sleights and charms and conventions – and our slave will stand revealed as our master, a brilliant example of nature's justice at work.

As for philosophy, it is all very well for adolescents, but it unfits grown men for the rough-and-tumble of practical life. Socrates should give it up before it is too late.

My dear Socrates – now don't be annoyed at what I'm going to say, for it is said out of kindness – don't you think it is really shameful to be what I think you are, and what others think you are, who are deeper philosophers? For now, if you or anyone like you were to be arrested on some charge, though you were totally innocent of any crime, do you realise that you wouldn't know what to do with yourself, but your head would spin and your mouth would drop open and not a word would come out of it? And into the dock you would go, and if your accuser – who might be the veriest good-for-nothing – if your accuser demanded it, you would get the death-sentence. What good can there be in an art which takes a man and turns him into less than a man, unable to protect himself or anyone else in time of peril, but hands him over to his enemies to strip naked – in short, makes him one who counts for nothing in his community [who is *atimos*, 'without *timé*']?

If Callicles was a real person it is rather surprising that such a forceful character has made no mark on history. He may only have been Plato's caricature of the typical selfish, narcissistic politician, but even so the caricature had a basis of fact.

In the early part of the fifth century, a hundred years before Plato wrote the *Gorgias*, Greece had owed the repulse of her invasion by the Persian Xerxes largely to the minds of two men, the Athenian Themistocles and the Spartan king Pausanias. The foresight of Themistocles had equipped the Athenians with a navy which could meet and beat the Persian navy at Salamis in 480 BC; as a result of which the isolated remnant of the Persian army could be defeated the next year by the combined Greek land forces under Pausanias, at Plataea.

When Pausanias, after the Plataean victory, surveyed the luxury of the enemy headquarters, he was amused that the Persians should have put at risk the riches they already had in order to plunder the poverty of the Greeks. But this child of the most impersonal state in Greece had caught an infection from his conquered foe. Pausanias began to see himself as an oriental despot like the Persian king, the one free man in a world of slaves. The golden tripod given to Apollo at Delphi to celebrate the victory he dedicated with a boastful inscription, as if it were his personal victory and his personal offering, and he a chieftain of the combined Greek forces like a second Agamemnon. His fellow-Spartans had the inscription erased, and substituted a list of the cities that had joined in the overthrow of the barbarian invader. Undeterred, Pausanias began to ape the manners and style of the enemy, and even to intrigue against his homeland with Xerxes. Finally he was recalled to Sparta, and was starved to death in a temple where he had sought asylum.

It is strange that his Athenian counterpart, Themistocles, followed a like course: self-aggrandisement which was suspected of aiming at tyranny, intrigue with Persia, and death in exile.

Athens was to experience the type again towards the end of the century, in the rich, foppish and brilliant Alcibiades, the favourite pupil of Socrates, and in another pupil of Socrates and uncle of Plato, Critias; one of those whose ruthless rule of Athens in the aftermath of her defeat by Sparta in the Peloponnesian War earned them the nickname of 'the thirty tyrants', and the bitter hatred of the democrats.

All these men were conscious seekers after personal power, different in kind from the earlier type of 'tyrant', who was flung up by a historical trend, as the champion of the people against the aristocracy.

That Alcibiades and Critias were encouraged by the new thought there can be no doubt (Critias was actually called a sophist). A contemporary, the comedian Aristophanes, regarded sophistry as a social blight, which taught men insubordination, and corrupted the young by causing them to 'wear out their backsides crouched on their haunches debating airy questions of no importance', instead of exercising in the gymnasium to become able-bodied citizens. How unlike their grandfathers, who had routed the army of Darius at Marathon, and smashed Xerxes's fleet at Salamis; those fine old salts whose talent for communication had been limited to 'shouting for their grub, crying, "yoho!"' as they heaved at their oar, and farting in the face of the rower behind'.

In the *Clouds* Aristophanes cast Socrates as the arch-villain in this piece; representing him both as a crack-pated physicist who had made his science into a new religion in which the law of Gravity had supplanted the law of God, and as an unscrupulous dialectician who taught his pupils – for a fee – how, by chopped logic, to make the worse appear the better cause.

Aristophanes was a genuine patriot, and in this sense a philotimous man of the older sort. But in another way he was closer than he thought to the sophists he attacked. His plays are full of criticism of his Athens, and are tinged with an individualism, but of a *laisser-faire* rather than of an assertive kind; a hankering after an ideal life in which the citizen is left alone by the politicians to enjoy life in his own way.

But what of Socrates himself? Was he an original philosopher, the relentless opponent of relativistic ethics, dishonest logic and meretricious oratory, as depicted by his admiring pupil Plato? Or was he in fact a corrupter of the youth, sowing doubts about the conventional morality and religion and undermining the foundations of society, as suggested by Aristophanes and asserted by those who had him condemned to drink the hemlock in 399 BC? Or was the man more nearly represented by that third picture, of an earthy, practical hater of cheats, humbugs and asses, whom he would cause, by ineluctable questioning as to their exact meaning, to expose themselves, in a manner which they considered indecent, and in the end intolerable?

Socrates left no writings of his own, and so must always remain something of an enigma. But the profound impact of his personality on others is a fact. Those who knew him said that he was like no other man, alive or dead; and moderns have seen in him the culmination or fruit of the whole growth of Greek culture that preceded him. This is true in a very interesting, if paradoxical, sense; for it is clear from all the ancient authorities that Socrates, though still a loyal citizen of Athens, yet cared nothing for *timé*: astonishing as it was for a Greek, he considered that to be mocked by his fellow-citizens for his eccentricity was 'no great matter'.

Granted this, the famous Socratic irony (for example, that the one thing he knew was that he knew nothing) is not hard to accept. We can be fairly certain of some other things too: that he saw himself as a sort of 'intellectual midwife', bringing to birth thoughts in his interlocutors' minds which were already there in embryo, by his process of succinct question and answer; and that for this he exacted no fee, as the sophists did. Also, that he was a practical man inasmuch as he saw everything in terms of means and ends – what is the end at which you are aiming, and is this the best way to achieve it? He also wanted definitions of words which seemed to him to be vague, and he thought that satisfactory definitions must be in terms of function (for example: you cannot properly define a saw without saying what it is supposed to do). In this he was only enunciating a basic assumption of his predecessors' world-view.

One question seems to have concerned him above all others:

what is *areté*, virtue, excellence? The *areté* of the Homeric hero had been to fight well and defend his community; the *areté* of a carpenter is to know the principles of woodworking, and to be able to put them into practice; the *areté* of the carpenter's saw is to cut wood, the task for which it was designed. There is no virtue in a saw which is blunt, as there is none in a carpenter who cannot tell a saw from a hammer. All around him in the world of 'nature' Socrates thought he detected a principle of function. But if it is the *areté* of the eyes to see, and of the teeth to bite, what is the *areté* of their owner, the man himself?

Socrates found that his fellow-Athenians attached the greatest importance to *areté*, and each wanted his sons to be taught it; but, on questioning them closely, he again and again discovered that not one of them knew what this prize was which they valued so highly. Neither did Socrates; but, as he would genially point out to his interlocutors, there was this difference between him and them – they thought that they knew, but he knew that he did not.

His self-confessed ignorance earned him from the Delphic Apollo the title of 'the wisest [it could be "the cleverest"] of men'. Over the entrance to the god's temple was inscribed the famous advice 'Know thyself'. This meant 'Know that you are a man and not a god', and Socrates deserved the divine congratulation on his recognition of his human limitations. But the god's behest could be understood in another way. For man to know himself he must know what is the function, the *areté* or virtue, of a human being. This is what Socrates could not discover, but one thing was clear to him: that, somehow, virtue must be knowledge. This conclusion seemed to have sanction both divine and human: divine, because Apollo ordered men to know themselves, and human, because Socrates's acquaintances all thought that virtue could be taught – and if it could be taught it must be knowable.

No wonder they killed him in the end. They killed him as animals or birds kill freaks born into their midst, or as Australian aborigines killed strangers who could not be covered by their book of etiquette. And Socrates undoubtedly was a freak. He was a loyal and devoted citizen of his city, and so should have fitted into the philotimous system; yet he despised *timé*, and that *areté* of which *timé* had been the putative recognition he saw, not as some parochial ability to benefit a man's own community, or as the selfish ability to gratify a man's own desires (like Callicles), but as the discharging of some function which he assumed to be common to human beings as human beings. Socrates likened himself to a midwife, who helped other men's ideas to birth. Others might liken him to a child which itself died in the throes of being born. I believe that the most significant side of this complex character emerged after his death, in a group of his followers to whom the so-called Cynics owed their origin.

The Cynics, the *canine* philosophers (*kynikos* = 'doggy') had as their father-founder one Antisthenes, a pupil of Socrates who admired particularly his master's impassivity and patience; his calmness under the pressure of emotional stress or physical hardship. His own biggest debt to philosophy, Antisthenes said, was that it taught him to 'talk to himself', to find his own company congenial. What a tale that tells of the distance some individuals had by now travelled from their society!

But it was a follower of Antisthenes who is most famed, in many an apocryphal anecdote, as the prototype of all Cynics: Diogenes, 'Socrates gone mad' (as Plato called him), who took up his quarters in a tub, mortified his flesh by rolling in hot sand in summer and embracing snow-covered statues in winter, told Alexander the Great not to block his sunlight, masturbated in the market-place, and otherwise offended the susceptibilities of worthy citizens, whom he castigated as being not men but mere slaves. A pupil of his, Crates, repulsive of aspect and intrusive of habit (he would enter private houses uninvited and treat the occupants to a personal harangue on their shortcomings), attracted the passion of Hipparchia, a girl of wealth and position, which she surrendered to become his wife and the only female Cynic. With him she joined in outraging the stuffy, assuming the grubby attire that was the intellectual's uniform, accompanying her husband to dinner-parties (a thing no decent Greek matron would have done), and giving earnests of their conjugal union in public, *more canino*, in true doggy fashion.

Diogenes used to say that all the conventional curses of Greek tragedy had been visited on him, for he was 'homeless, stateless, bereft of country, a vagabond and a beggar, living from hand to mouth.' Of all these, ultimate terrors to the philotimous man, he was actually boasting, just as he was boasting when he confessed to having 'defaced the currency'.

This confession was taken literally by later ages (who added that he had been exiled for the offence), but Diogenes was speaking metaphorically. When he said he was defacing the currency he meant that he was attacking convention, the basis of society. And he was expressing this most forcibly, by using the metaphor of the currency, the oil of the wheels of society, which, though appearing to have a value in itself, has in fact no value except that given it by convention (*nomos*, so the Greek for 'coinage', 'currency', is *nomisma*).

In the controversy between nature, *physis*, and convention or custom, *nomos*, then, the Cynics were firmly on the side of *physis*. This was the point of the Cynics' 'shamelessness'. They were 'doing what comes naturally', and rejoiced to do it in a way that flouted etiquette and disgusted respectable citizens, to whom they were giving a sort of practical sermon. For they thought that *areté* consisted in 'following nature', and in deeds rather than in words. But the nature to be followed is not our own individual desires or whims (as a Callicles would have it), but a principle in the universe ('Mother Nature' almost, by now!) of minimal requirements for survival. What need of a mansion to keep out the rain, when a hole (or a tub) will do as well? Or what need of fine raiment, when an old coat will keep you as warm? Such elaborations are mere status symbols of *conventional* societies. Follow nature conceived in this way, and you will be as self-sufficient as man can be, a *virtuous* man, the image of God, who is wholly self-sufficient.

The lesson the Cynics taught was that natural man is an autonomous individual. There was a story that Diogenes was being sold into slavery. When asked what skill he had, he replied 'man-management', and told the dealer to look for buyers who wanted to buy themselves a master. He meant that really he was free, and they the slaves – of convention. The Cynic was the citizen of no single city, but of the world; to him, all men were fellow-citizens, and all war is civil war (and to the philotimous man civil war was the ultimate abomination).

In this way the Cynics had moved beyond their inspiration, Socrates. That process of the birth of the individual (or *private*) person – so long in gestation – which was begun with him, was completed with them. (It is noteworthy that it is with the Cynics that we first meet with the metaphor of the role, *persona*, assumed by the individual in society.) And, having been born into the world of action, this new personal being was spread in society by *contagion*.

To call this new phenomenon 'better' than the soil in which it had grown would, I think, be unfair. Without the type of the philotimous man, who was the product of a sort of dialectic of social history, his antitype, the *aphilotimous* man, adumbrated by Socrates and advertised by the Cynics, could never have happened. Yet, if not better than the philotimous man, the aphilotimous man was certainly different from him; and if this difference was not a mere logical distinction, but a real one, it must have been a difference in his capacity for experience – or rather, the way in which he experienced things, the quality of his experiences.

Analogies have their uses, though those who are most acquainted with the habits of these beasts know that they can be as dangerous as metaphors and must not be pressed too far. The analogy I wish gingerly to parade now is that of the casting of sculpture, where the artist first models the figure to be cast, which becomes the core of the matrix or mould solidified about it, wherein the features of the model are reproduced in reverse. The philotimous man would correspond to the model, and his aphilotimous antitype to the mould, which could never have existed without him. Or you might prefer a more reflective analogy: your image in the mirror would not exist without you, and it looks human enough to the uncritical, although closer inspection will reveal that your right side and your left side have changed places.

Analogies apart, the essential novelty about this new kind of man was his lack of *philotimia*. This was a portent which cannot be underestimated. The process of individuation within a society, a process which had been shaped and energised by the twin instruments of *thymos* and *philotimia*, had cast up a kind of individual in whom the mainspring of social action (and indeed social progress) – *philotimia* – was missing. These individuals may have regarded themselves as more godlike than their fellows; yet they still had to live together. But what is it that binds, moves and guides a *divine* community?

3

The God Within

There is no doubt what guided the community of Homer's gods, even if it hardly sustained that community, and certainly did not bind it: *philotimia*. It is improbable that Homer was the first to liken gods to men, but it is not impossible that he was the first to do it with such a vengeance. His gods are super-human rather than divine, they are his heroes writ large; actuated by *philotimia* without being restrained by shame, as the heroes were, from breaking the rules of the game.

On the topmost peak of Mount Olympus, above the rain-clouds and the snowstorms, stood the brazen-floored palace of Zeus, surrounded by those of his children, which had been built for them by the craft of Hephaestus. These palaces were like the palaces of human royalty, just as the gods' temples on earth were modelled on the hall of an earthly king. It was in Zeus's hall that they would foregather, sometimes to take counsel but more often to take wine. There, bathed in perpetual sunlight, they feasted, pledged each other in golden goblets, diverted them-selves with watching the antics of humanity below, and quarrelled jealously about each one's due of *timé* from men.

'It must have been the hell of a heaven' remarked Stephen Leacock, prompted by one such domestic scene on Olympus; a scene which shows how the society of the *Iliad*'s gods reflects the society of a primitive aristocracy. The poet tells how the quarrel of Achilles and Agamemnon on earth led to a quarrel between Zeus and his queen in heaven; and how, in an attempt to pour oil on the troubled waters, the lame Hephaestus proposed that he fetch everyone a drink. Tension was relieved, 'and the gods laughed uproariously to see him stumping busily through the hall'.

What annoyed Leacock was that Homer's gods should find physical deformity funny. His condemnation was just, yet also austere. In a warrior society physical disability excuses one from fighting, without the disgrace of cowardice, and enables one to use one's quieter talents for the general good (as an architect of their houses Hephaestus was welcomed seriously enough by his fellow-gods). It also licenses one to castigate the values of the society to whose fringe one has been relegated, like the fool or jester, because one does not appear to be a threat to anyone else's *philotimia*. Hephaestus has the humanity of the jester; Aeschylus felt the humanity, or humaneness, of this god's character, when he cast him as the reluctant executioner of Zeus's sentence on the philanthropist Prometheus.

The gods' *philotimia* was mainly served by the sacrifices and burnt-offerings which men made to them (satirists were later to suggest that a moratorium on these might starve heaven into submission). They were jealous of each other, and easily offended. The hatred of Hera and Athena for Troy was unrelenting, because the Trojan Paris had awarded the prize for beauty against them, to the goddess of love, Aphrodite. On the other hand, Hera's husband Zeus valued Troy above all other cities, because his altar there 'never lacked its due portion of sacrifice'. Nevertheless, for the sake of domestic peace he surrendered his devotees to his queen's anger, 'of his own free will, but against his inclination'. Only let fair be fair: if, he said, *he* should ever want to wipe out some favourite city of hers, she must not try to stand in his way.

Zeus presided over his unruly family as a genial and (on the whole) indulgent patriarch, with an eye for a pretty girl; a weakness for which he was prepared to put up with a certain amount of hen-pecking. Compared with humans, he and his divine company were in some respects behind the times, even *sub*-human; but there were other respects in which he was ahead of them, as we shall see.

On occasion, the Father of gods and men could become exasperated with the Olympians' persistent interference in human affairs on behalf of their favourites, which could have the effect of thwarting his own intention; and the gods shook in their golden sandals at the direness of his warning.

Hear what I have to say, gods and goddesses, and respect

it. If I see any of you sneaking off to help either side, Trojans or Greeks, his homecoming will be a sorry and a sore one. I will take him and hurl him into the murk of Tartarus, where the gulf below the earth yawns deepest behind iron gates set in a brazen porch, as far beneath the dwellings of the dead as the heavens are above the dwellings of the living; then he will know whether any god can match my might or no.

If you are incredulous, why, test me for yourselves. Hang a golden rope from the sky and heave on it, all of you, gods and goddesses: strain as you might, you would not tumble king Zeus out of his heaven. But if I should choose to give a counterheave, I could pull you all up, yes, and earth and sea with you. Then I would hitch the rope round a crag of Olympus, and leave the lot dangling. This is the measure of my superiority, whether above gods or above men.

Just as the *timé* due to the gods was greater than that due to men, so the gods' *areté*, virtue, was greater than men's. This is another sign that divine society in the poem reflects the human; for the Olympians feared threats from no enemies, and they had therefore no real need of the Homeric brand of virtue. But though they were bigger and stronger than men, and could do things which men could not, such as fly through the air, change their shapes, or make themselves or their favourite humans invisible, they were lacking in some of the things we should expect of deity, for they were not omnipresent or omniscient (prayers might go unheard, because they were away having dinner with the Ethiopians), and the omnipotence of even Zeus himself was in doubt, as subordinate to Fate.

Yet the really fundamental difference between the gods and us men was that they do not wear out with the years and die: they are 'deathless and ageless'. Plato was to define death as the 'separation of soul (*psyché*) and body', and a god as a being with soul and body, but in whom the two were as it were fused into one inseparable entity. Homer never speaks of the gods as having 'soul' at all, though his men have it; its presence in them makes them alive.

Homer's treatment of his gods contained a considerable

element of humour. The fun was lost on one Xenophanes, a much-travelled Greek from Asia Minor, who was writing in the latter part of the sixth and early fifth centuries. Homer and Hesiod, he complained, made the gods thieve, cheat and whore – behaviour that would be considered outrageous in a mere man. Those old poets were exaggerating a tendency which he noted as universal: the tendency of men to make gods in their own image. African gods were black and snubnosed, those of northerners redhaired and blue-eyed. If animals had any artistic ability, lions would depict the gods as lions, horses would depict them as equine, and so on.

Xenophanes goes on to reveal the truth of the matter.

> There is one god, greatest among gods and men, unlike men in shape or intellect. He sees and hears and apprehends with the whole of himself. He does not need to stir, but moves everything by the deliberations of his mind.

It looks as if this trend towards monotheism is linked with the beginnings of philosophy, which was born in Xenophanes's own Ionia, and was not much older than he. As I have said, the fundamental shift of viewpoint which distinguished the philosophical from the mythical account of the world was that, where myth had seen all natural things as interrelated because they have a common ancestry, philosophy saw them as interrelated because they are all made of the same stuff: all the variety of the phenomena is to be explained as diverse modifications of a common substance.

Now if such a substance exists, underlying all the changes of the universe, though its modifications are transient – are born and die (as common parlance has it) – yet it itself must be indestructible, and last for ever. But indestructibility is precisely the quality which marks off the divine from the non-divine, the immortal from the mortal; therefore this substance is god, and the stuff of everything is divine and deathless.

Though Xenophanes's supreme god perhaps owes a lot to contemporary ideas of a universal, divine substance, he is not however to be identified with that substance. He is rather a divine mind, governing his universe far and wide without the locomotion that a body would need to oversee each part, with perceptions, wisdom, power and (we may infer) moral character more perfect than those of the Homeric Zeus.

The suggestion had already been made by the time of Xenophanes, that this common substance of all things is air. A contemporary of his, another Ionian, Heraclitus, proposed a more exciting element, fire. His reasons can be guessed at: fire is potentially ubiquitous, it comes mysteriously into being anywhere – yet something cannot come from nothing (Lear's 'nothing will come of nothing' has a long ancestry); warmth is the agent, nurse and inseparable companion of life; and the flickering flames have the darting restlessness of thought.

The basis of the universe, then, is an 'everliving fire, kindled in measures and quenched in measures', which is also 'soul', *psyché*, and 'the principle of order', *logos*; 'the only wise (*or* clever) thing' ('the supreme craftsman' would not be far off), which 'both accepts and rejects the name of Zeus'.

This last quotation is a good example of Heraclitus's dark and riddling way of expressing himself, through paradoxical apophthegms: to describe this active intelligence of which the world is constituted by the name of 'Zeus' is to convey some notion of its majesty, yet is also to circumscribe and limit something which is unlimited and beyond human comprehension altogether. Men contradict each other; God is nothing if not self-contradictory. Heraclitus explained universal change as the result of a tension of opposites (a sort of cosmic tug-of-war), like the tension which gives its efficaciousness to the string of a bow or of a musical instrument. 'Homer was a fool,' he said, 'when he prayed that war and strife might perish from among us'; for strife is life.

Search as you may, said Heraclitus, you will never find the limits of Soul, 'so profound is its structure'. This is a far cry from the soul in Homer, where it is hardly mentioned except when it leaves the body at death, or nearly leaves it in a faint. It is the vital principle, 'the breath of life', the presence of which distinguishes the living from the dead (corpses do not breathe). Etymologically it is related to a verb meaning 'to cool' or 'to air', and Plato was probably not far out when he interpreted *psyché* as 'that which ventilates the body'.

To Homer, as to his forebears, the utter annihilation of life would have been unthinkable, so that for him souls must persist after their departure from their bodies: but equally unthinkable was the idea that there could be any real life for the individual apart from his body. His body, the instrument of his sensual delight in life, was the man. The proem of the *Iliad* announces the poem's theme, the destructive anger of Achilles, which 'sent the souls of many heroes to the house of Hades, but themselves it made the prey of dogs and carrion birds'; the flesh that is torn, and the bones that are crunched, are more nearly the heroes' *selves* than the shadowy souls of them, rushing to the 'vasty hall of Death'.

When the ghost of Patroclus appeared to Achilles in a dream, pleading with his friend to provide its body with a proper burial, Achilles started out of his sleep with a cry of surprise. 'So even in the underworld,' he exclaimed, 'there is a soul and image of the man, but it is utterly witless [or perhaps "gutless"]'. The soul flutters and squeaks feebly like a bat, it cannot help itself, but must commission the strength of the living even to bring it duly to the palace of Hades, the Keeper of the Dead.

But when it gets there, what awaits it? A limbo of infinite boredom. When Odysseus went, in the eleventh book of the *Odyssey*, to consult the oracular dead at the dark confines of Ocean and Erebus, he met the souls of many who had fought by his side on the plain of Troy. One was the soul of Achilles, cut short in the flower of his youth. Odysseus politely tried to console him, remarking that he seemed to have quite as much honour among the shades as he had had on earth. But the ghost replied, sternly: 'Do not play down death to me, Odysseus. I would rather be the hired servant of a man with no land and little livelihood in the world above, than lord of all the dead.' To the Homeric hero, aristocrat though he was, a tramp who still saw the light of the sun would be the envy of a dead king.

Death was an unpleasant necessity. A mortal, even a hero, was not expected to welcome it, but he was expected to meet the inevitable without fuss, and as nobly as possible, showing that the *timé* he had had in life was not undeserved. This point, that to be immortal is better but, being mortal, to do the duty that is expected of us is the best course open to us, is strikingly put by the Lycian King Sarpedon to Glaucus, in a passage from the *Iliad* which I have already used. I quote it again, and here add its significant conclusion.

Glaucus, why are you and I honoured above all others in Lycia with the highest places at table and the best meat and full cups? Why do all regard us as if we were gods, and allot to us especially a great estate of rich tilth and ploughed land by the banks of the Xanthus? It is so that we should now stand in the forefront of the Lycians and face searing battle; and so that the Lycian warriors may say, 'Certainly our leaders are not inglorious, who rule in Lycia and eat fine meat and drink choice wine: they deserve it, for their valour too is exceptional, as they fight in the forefront of the Lycian army'.

My friend, if our reward for surviving this war were to be freedom from old age and death, you would not find me in the front rank, nor would I be coaxing you into battle, the breeding-ground of glory. But as, whatever we do, death stands about us in ten thousand shapes, and no mortal can escape or dodge it, come, let us find if some foe will give us aught to boast about, or we him.

For many years this attitude of hopelessness prevailed; but the sixth century, which brought the first philosophers with their new idea of a deity incorporated into the physical universe, saw also the birth of another, less intellectual, phenomenon: the spread of the so-called mystery religions.

Essentially, a brighter promise, of association or communion with a god, was offered by these mystery religions to their initiates. The two most important cults were those of the god Dionysus (or Bacchus) and the goddess Demeter, neither of them members of the Olympian pantheon of Homer, who hardly notices them. The poet did know of the retribution visited on a brash king, who made a murderous assault with an ox-goad on the nurses of the 'raving Dionysus', causing consternation to them and terror to the god, who dived into the sea to escape; but this is about all he seems to know.

This story may have suggested to Euripides the plot of his savage and beautiful play *The Bacchantes*, written shortly before he died, in his seventies, in 407 BC. The play tells how Pentheus, the self-confident young king of Thebes, is worried by the appearance in his city of an enigmatic stranger from Asia, with a troupe of female followers, who is fascinating the Theban womenfolk with uncouth and unseemly rites out on the hillside. The stranger is in fact Dionysus, *incognito*, attended by his Maenads ('Ravers'), and in the play he visits with a terrible punishment the mortal who tries to suppress his gospel. Like the 'devil' of a witches' coven, the god is the only male among the band of female celebrants, whom he leads coursing over the mountain slopes, partners in his wild abandon and ecstatic chase which will culminate in the seizing, rending and devouring of some terrified goat. Euripides's Maenads describe this orgiastic euphoria in their choral songs, of which the following may serve as a sample – though shorn, I fear, of the stirring poetry and spinning rhythm.

What joy he gives when from the running band of mountain revellers he drops to the ground in the grip of ecstasy, he, the wearer of the fawnskin vestment, the hunter after the draught of goat's blood and the savour of raw flesh, pressing on at the head of our rout to the Phrygian mountains or the hills of Lydia – Bromios the Bellower! Whoopee! See, see how from the earth there wells up for us milk, and wine, and the nectar of bees!

See how our Bacchus brandishes aloft the blaze of his resinous torch, and makes the smoke stream from it as if of Syrian frankincense, as he revives flagging spirits with his whirling dance or jolts them with his yells and tosses his sleek locks to the winds! And midst the yells he thunders, 'On, Maenads, on! Gold-flowing Tmolus has equipped you – so hymn Dionysus with the roll of drums, and with whoopee and babble delight the god of whoopee, while the reedy flute sounds *holy! holy! holy!* in time with our race, in time with our race to the mountains!'

Then, then, what delight, as she plies her swift limbs in the whirl of the dance, like a frolicsome foal at the side of its pasturing dam in the mead, to the Maenad!

By Euripides's time the cult had been opened to men as well

as women, and it had become formalised, respectable and staid. Even so, the ladies still went hill-trekking occasionally; as late as the first century AD we hear of such an expedition, which was marooned on the summit of Parnassus by a blizzard, and had to be rescued by the husbands. Indeed, a remnant of the Dionysiac mystery may still be with us today, embodied in a strange festival at Monoklissia, a village in northern Greece, where once a year the women 'put on the trousers' and take over the cafés, drinking, smoking and gambling, while their men are condemned within doors to a day of housework. Then woe betide any male who dares to show his nose out! He is stripped, drenched with ice-water, and fined to help pay for the climax of the festival, 'an all-night, women-only revel at the local tavern. Several lambs and chickens are slaughtered for the occasion, and large quantities of wine stocked for the feast. Yet no one seems to know what goes on behind the locked doors of the tavern. The only man allowed in is the aged bagpipe player, who sits there playing blindfold all night.'

The cult appears to have originated in Asia Minor, and to have reached the Greeks by way of the Thracian wilds to the north of them. In the middle of the sixth century BC, perhaps coincident with its spread to the more civilised centres of southern Greece, an attempt was made to give it a sort of intellectual respectability. A literary forgery appeared in Athens, a poem ascribed to an early victim of the Thracian Maenads, the legendary musician Orpheus, whose art had melted the wrath of lions and moved oak-trees to dance, and

> Whom Universal nature did lament,
> When by the rout that made the hideous roar,
> His goary visage down the stream was sent,
> Down the swift *Hebrus* to the *Lesbian* shore.

Orpheus could therefore pass as something of an authority on the religion of Bacchus, and 'his' poem purported to explain the barbaric ritual of the dismemberment and eating of the goat as the symbolic re-enactment of a myth about the god. According to this, the young Dionysus was once given into the safe-keeping of the earthborn Titans. But as the child was playing with its toys, these *farouche* nursemaids set upon it, tore it to pieces, and ate of it. For this dereliction of duty they were thunderbolted by Zeus; the immortal child of course came to no lasting harm, but from the ashes of the Titans sprang Man, who as a result has a dual nature, compounded of Titanic violence and a portion of divinity, gained by our forebears' consumption of the divine flesh. Initiation into his cult enhances this divinity, this relationship with the god, and induces a true communion with him.

Much gentler was the cult of the goddess of the cornfields, Demeter, and her daughter Persephone, the consort of the Keeper of the Dead. At first it had been a merely local one, at Eleusis, a few miles from Athens, but in the middle of the sixth century interest in it, as in the cult of Dionysus, had become much more widespread. The Eleusinian temple was greatly extended, to include a Hall of Initiation.

The blessings conferred upon her initiates by Demeter were less immediate than those of Dionysus: they were to be reaped in the next life rather than in this. They are summed up in some lines of a hymn to the goddess written in the springtime of her popularity: 'Blessed is the man who has looked upon these rites; but no such portion of blessings awaits one who enters the shadowy world of death an uninitiated outsider'; or, as it was put a century later, 'Thrice blessed are those who go to the House of Hades having witnessed these ceremonies; for they alone have the gift of life beyond the grave, while for the others all is wretchedness'.

Initiates will be fit to associate with the deities in the world to come; but these passages do not threaten the uninitiated with actual punishment in that world – rather with the miserable, unrelieved boredom which to Homer was the fate of all souls as they eke out their twilight existence in Hades. The initiated soul, on the other hand, will be a robust entity, truly alive and capable of that zestful enjoyment, in divine company, of the good things which Homer depicts his Olympians as always enjoying. Salvation, for the devotees of Demeter, consisted in a never-ending festivity in the best company; as Plato put it sardonically, the evangelists of these mysteries promise their followers full-blooded pleasures in the after-life, 'conducting them in imagination to a banquet of the saints in the house of

Hades, where they sit them down all garlanded and make them tipsy for ever – reckoning the fairest reward for virtue to be eternal drunkenness.'

Those who had 'looked upon the mysteries of Demeter' and had been let into the secret were forbidden to disclose it; and they kept their trust so well that we know little of the actual rite of initiation. Probably the neophyte underwent a token rebirth, as we hear that among the sacred implements was a symbolic vagina (like the Hindu *yoni*), through which he or she might have to pass. Ceremonial purity was demanded of the participants, for to be admitted to a god's company one must be clean; and there is no purity like that of the new-born. A story by J. G. Frazer is in point here, of the Indian ambassadors who had been so polluted by their visit to England that on their return to their own country nothing would serve but for them to be born again. 'For the purpose of regeneration it is directed to make the image of pure gold of the female power of nature, in the shape either of a woman or of a cow. In this statue the person to be regenerated is enclosed, and dragged through the usual channel.' As this is expensive, a more formalised ceremony, passage through the sacred *yoni*, was considered sufficient to remove ordinary taints, but in this extreme case the rajah ordered a gold statue to be made, and his emissaries were dragged through it.

Both Dionysus and Demeter were deities of vegetation, Dionysus of the vine and Demeter of the corn; and the phenomenon of vegetable growth, decay and renewal easily intertwines with the idea of the rebirth of the individual. The vegetable world is a handy exemplar of continuity interrupted, or repetition – but continuity of what? and repetition of what? In what sense can an *individual* be interrupted, or repeated? Is not the individual plant's sole function to carry the seed of its successor, which when it has done it is finished? A shift of emphasis is taking place; an individual *god* (something perfect or complete) is being interrupted or repeated – or else something is being given, with each rebirth, another chance to improve upon itself. But *improve* – what does that mean, in this context? Another chance to learn from, and not to repeat, past mistakes? Mistakes about what?

Ordinary men of that time would have had no answers to such questions, which they would not have thought to ask. But to one extraordinary man, Pythagoras of Samos, an answer had occurred: that which continues is not 'family' or 'species', but an immortal soul, and the interruptions of its career are no more than changes of abode, when it departs at death from one body to animate the embryo of another. This is his famous doctrine of reincarnation, or metempsychosis. Tales were told of Pythagoras's own reincarnations: how he had once been a Trojan, and fought alongside Hector, and how, even earlier, he had been a son of the god Hermes, who had promised to grant him one wish – for anything except for immortality. So Pythagoras, with Greek astuteness, asked that his soul, whether it were among the living or the dead, should remember all that happened to it; a condition hardly to be distinguished from personal immortality, if the continuity of 'selfhood' is to be defined as a continuing strand of memory. The soul of Pythagoras became immune to the effects, or the blessings, of Lethe, the river of forgetfulness, of which all souls must drink in the next world.

Early evidence for the life and teachings of this enigmatic personage is scanty, though traditions about him in later ages are plentiful. Amidst the growth of this tradition romance luxuriated, but that it had its roots in fact there is no need to doubt, and we can use it judiciously to discern, through the mists, something of the historical figure of Pythagoras.

His life largely spanned the sixth century BC; that is, he was contemporary with the invigoration and spread of the mystery religions, into the secrets of some at least of which he had been initiated. Perhaps he found them wanting; anyway, in his native island of Samos, off the coast of Asia Minor, he established a brotherhood, a guild of 'friends', who called themselves by a new name, *philosophers*, 'lovers of *sophia*' (a word usually, though not very adequately, translated as 'wisdom'). The members of this brotherhood would not 'see death'.

Pythagoras had founded a new mystery religion, conceived in a marriage of the already existent mystery cults with the nascent physical science of Ionia. He knew of the search which was going on just across the water for some single substance underlying all nature. It had been revealed to him that this single underlying substance of all things was not water, or air, or fire, but *number*.

For he had discovered that a physical fact, the attunement of a musical stringed instrument, is expressible mathematically; a musical interval – which is a physical fact because it is recognisable by the ear – can be put as a numerical proportion, of 2 : 1 for the interval of the octave, and so on. Indeed, every physical object is measurable; but why? Because everything is *made* of number, of course! The whole universe is made of number, and of numerical proportions (or, as the Greeks called them, harmonies)!

From very early times the name of Pythagoras has been linked with the science of mathematics. For most worldlings our first (perhaps our only) meeting with Himself used to be our introduction to the forty-seventh theorem in the first book of Euclid, 'Pythagoras's' proof that the square on the hypotenuse of a right-angled triangle is equal to the sum of the squares of the other two sides. Later legend made him sacrifice an ox (or even a hundred oxen) in gratitude for the apperception of this proof; an apocryphal story, for the Euclidean demonstration would have been beyond the mathematical comprehension of the historical Pythagoras. Yet I can fancy the historical Pythagoras being moved to make a thank-offering to heaven when the much more catholic and important intuition was vouchsafed to him, of the fundamental *cosmic* importance of Number; I can fancy too that the sacrificial animal (hardly a hundred of them) was made of dough, as some ancient authorities tell us, consistently with that gentle soul's abhorrence of bloodshed.

It was no doubt a crudity to suppose that, because physical facts are expressible in number, things must actually be made of number, and that number is of the same order as water or air. To us, who look back at it all through the lens of later logic (a lens which itself may not be entirely flawless) the absurdity is patent; but Pythagoras could still have appreciated that he had had an insight of superlative importance, even if he did not also appreciate its myriad ramifications; and this struck him with the force of a divine revelation. He was the recipient of the final mystery: the universal God was not what the physicists had so far thought him to be, not even what he has since been called – a mathematician – but Number; or rather an ultimate blend of all numbers, the supreme harmony, yet (like Xenophanes's God) intelligent and active. The later assertion is quite credible, that Pythagoras raised mathematics from the market-place, from the constriction of simply being able to count one's change, to the status of the supreme *sophia* – 'skill', 'technique', 'science' (if you will), even 'wisdom' here – acquired by appreciation of the orderly dance, the harmonious interrelations, of the universe in all its parts; a harmony taken for granted by the simple, overlooked by the sophisticated, but awesome to the thoughtful, even if they call it Chance rather than God.

Centuries later the doctor Galen was to observe that contemplation of the universe was to 'strike the layman with its beauty, and the scientist with its subtlety'. In Pythagoras layman and scientist were still indistinguishable; indistinguishable to him were beauty and subtlety (he it was who, traditionally, gave the name of *kosmos* – 'order' or 'ornament' ['beauty'] to the universe); he felt the pride and the humility of one who had glimpsed an answer to the question 'How can the one be many?' – what is it that unifies the diversity of things, in what way is the complex also simple?

Whom would such a vision not force to his knees? What man would feel that he was worthy to receive it? We are not surprised to be told that Pythagoras exacted a ritual purity from his followers with whom he shared his secret. As the years go on, the imagined details of this 'way of life' are elaborated; but attested early enough are abstention from bloodshed, vegetarianism, and an extraordinary curb upon the tongue, a formal silence demanded of the neophyte; as if we are on the threshold of a refinement of the idea of impurity; 'not that which goeth into the mouth defileth a man; but that which cometh out of the mouth, this defileth a man'.

If Pythagoras wrote anything at all, it was soon lost. More probably he wrote nothing, but was one of those few who, by their mere presence and the force of their living word, have tilted the tiller at a critical point in Psyche's course. What we think we know of the Master's own teaching is inference, based on second-hand circumstantial evidence, and an assumption that the source of such a rich smoke could only have been an exceptionally brilliant fire. To later tradition his austere serenity, his miraculous powers over nature, his uncanny insights into secrets hidden from ordinary men by the gramarye of time and space – all these made him into something super-human, if not actually into a god (there were those who identified him with the Hyperborean Apollo, from the paradise beyond the North Wind).

But of another bizarre person, close to Pythagoras in time and thought, we are fortunate in possessing considerable first-hand knowledge. Empedocles was born soon after 500 BC into a rich family at Sicilian Acragas (the modern Agrigento). While still a young man he appears to have joined a Pythagorean society in the town, and to have become conscious that he had a mission to humanity. He embodied his gospel – the dissemination of which took him to many a Greek city – in a poem called *Purifications*, of which sufficient fragments survive to give us a good idea of the contents.

A clue to the meaning of the work's title is given by an ancient authority who tells us that Empedocles 'taught that souls are divine, and those men are divine too who partake of them in all purity'. The phraseology, with its implied distinction between the soul and the man whose body it inhabits, will ring less oddly when we recall the distinction which Homer too made between the heroes themselves and their souls. But there is a further implication: that the impurity, which debars a man from divinity, is in him rather than in the already divine soul which accompanies him. Cleanse ourselves of this impurity, whatever it is, and shall we not merge with our 'soul-mate', to partake of its divinity? John or Jane Smith, whose body had been the temporary and evanescent vehicle of this uncanny sojourner, will merge and be identified with it, to enjoy its godhead – and this consummation is expressed symbolically, or poetically, or mythologically, under the image of the ability to remember previous incarnations.

But to Empedocles the taint of impurity had been incurred by the divine soul of itself. This he knew by personal experience and recollection, the credentials of his testimony.

There is a matter of Necessity, [he says] an ancient decree of the gods, eternal and sealed with broad oaths: that whenever one of the deities, whose lot is length of life, sins and defiles himself with bloodshed, and, siding with Strife, perjures himself, then he must wander for thrice ten thousand seasons away from the company of the blessed ones, taking in the course of time all kinds of mortal shapes, exchanging one painful way of life for another. For the mighty air chases him into the sea, but the sea spews him out on to the dry earth, the earth into the rays of the sun, and this plunges him back into the eddying air. One element takes him from another, but all hate him. Such a one am I now, an exile and wanderer from the gods, I who trusted in mad Strife.

From this we gather that Empedocles regarded himself as a divinity; that the company of his fellow-gods had bound itself by oath not to quarrel; that the penalty for transgressing this oath was exile for a period to this world of mutability and discord, to suffer reincarnations in various bodies; that he himself was such a transgressor, and such an exile; and – by implication – that other such exiles are in our midst, imprisoned in the bodies of some, if not all, of us (otherwise why should he bother to spread his message?).

Other fragments of his poem graphically describe the banished soul's entry into this world, its first view of the scene of its punishment: a dark cave, how unlike the high estate (*timé*) and wealth of blessings it has left! – a dark meadow, misruled by Mischief, the haunt of all sorts of ghoulish powers, Anger, Murder, Disease and Decay: 'I wept and shrieked,' he says, 'when I saw the uncongenial place', as a new-born baby heralds its arrival with a yell premonitory of sorrows to come.

The ultimate symbol of strife is the slaughter of one living thing by another, which is a sort of civil or familial war; yet even here on earth there was once a Golden Age, ruled over not by Zeus or Ares the god of war, but by the Cyprian goddess of love; then there was no killing, no bloodshed, men propitiated the gods not with bloody sacrifices but with offerings of honey and pictures of beasts – for of all abominations the most hideous was to 'smash the life out of a creature and then to bury one's teeth in its lovely limbs'; then all creation lived at peace with itself, animals were tame and well-disposed to mankind, and everywhere 'glowed the warmth of good-fellowship'.

Perhaps Empedocles claimed to owe his account of the Golden Age to personal recollection, for he says that he has seen many reincarnations (and indeed he seems now to have reached the end of the cycle): 'I myself have been a man and a woman, a plant, a bird, and a dumb fish of the sea.'

The promise which Empedocles appears to hold out to those who will listen to him is of a remission of sentence: by following his teaching, and by returning to the way of friendship which we once abandoned, of escape from the cycle of rebirth before the full period of 'thirty thousand seasons' has elapsed. The reformed prisoner can win himself better and better prison-houses, better and better reincarnations. He will exchange the circle of rebirths for a spiral, as it were, and this will lead to the longed-for escape back to the heavenly society he once knew.

Quaintly, Empedocles grades the excellence of incarnations. Among plants it is best to be Apollo's laurel, among 'beasts that couch on the mountainside' a lion; but best among men are 'seers and songsters and healers and champions of humankind', general benefactors, indeed, as Empedocles himself now is. From there, their next step is to godhead: 'Thereafter they burgeon into gods most reverend, to share hearth and table with the other gods, exempt from the woes and weariness of men', beyond the numbing effect of 'bliss and teen'.

To join, or to *re*join, the gods? I have suggested that Empedocles must have thought that all, or at least some, of us entertain within us a 'demonic' or divine 'soul', with which our own selves can merge. Yet such fragments of the *Purifications* as we possess can be interpreted in a different way: as the revelation by a god of the secret of godhead, as teaching Man to become something he is not, that is, God.

If this is the correct interpretation of Empedocles, then he was indeed a very extraordinary person – or at least a very extra-ordinary Greek, for as I have remarked the Greeks had taken it for granted that lions are produced by lions, heroes by heroes, gods by gods, and men by men. One is god or man *physei*, by origin or 'nature', and there is no transition from one nature (or one class) to another. Like to like, never like to unlike; this was a principle of Greek thought. In the Dionysiac myth, man can assimilate godhead because man is physically related to God, he has some of the essence of God already in him. There seems to be an ambiguity here, parallel to the ambiguity whether *areté* is implanted in a man by birth (or origin, or nature), *physei*, or whether it can be acquired by learning. It is the ambiguity of adoption: is the adopted a mere recruit to swell the number of supporters of the family interest, or does he, through the ceremony of adoption, acquire some ancestral quality or virtue of the family, some special *areté*?

If Empedocles were teaching that man can be transmuted into something he is not, into God, then he might be called the first *psychochemist*: for this change would find an analogy in chemical change. Some psychic compound with new qualities or properties, which its antecedents or constituents did not of themselves possess, could come into being. Extraordinary as it would be, it is not impossible that this was his teaching, for in another work of his, which was known by the title *On Nature*, he actually propounded a doctrine of 'chemical change'. As the basic stuff of the physical universe he postulated, not the single element of the Ionians or Pythagoras, but the famous four – fire, air, earth, water – which, while being themselves irreducible data, or 'immortal', formed the transient objects of the physical world by combining with each other in different proportions. For example, if they were mixed in a certain proportion, 'bonded by the glue of Harmony in divinely wondrous wise', bone would come into being; change the proportion, the 'harmony', and the result would be something different – say, flesh or blood. The change which Empedocles imagines his elements as undergoing beneath the wand of Harmony (no more silly a personification than 'Nature' or other purposeful or provident abstractions which others since him have used) is an adumbration of chemical change.

Such an idea, skirting as it does the need for fixed classes or species in nature, opens the door to that of evolution, and Empedocles did propound a theory of the chance 'survival of the fittest' which anticipated Darwin in a quite remarkable way. One would hardly have expected such fluid concepts as those

of chemical change and evolution to appeal to an aristrocrat,
such as we know Empedocles to have been; but apparently his
politics were as odd as his philosophy, for he favoured the democratic faction in Acragas. More orthodox was an elder contemporary, the poet Pindar, who certainly did not see the soul as
the product of any evolutionary process, but as an uncanny
stranger (or semi-stranger) whom we harbour within us.

When you are awake, he says, your soul lies dormant; but
when you lose consciousness your soul comes into its own, and
signals truth to you in a way that transcends time and space.
'The body of everyone obeys the behest of imperious death. But
there yet endures a quick image of the living creature; for that
alone is from the gods. When the limbs are active, it sleeps; but
to the sleeper, in many a dream, it foreshadows the approaching
issue of joy or sorrow.' The soul comes from the gods, and for
this reason it lasts on when the body perishes, and is untram-
melled by the limitations which set bounds to knowledge gained
through the bodily senses. It has two characteristics of its divine
source, immortality and the power of divination.

Further (and no doubt more rational) evidence for man's
kinship with God was seen in our possession of reason. Man
alone among living things worships gods, or indeed distinguishes
them as something other than himself; he alone can understand
the orderliness of the cosmos, this device contrived by a master
engineer – because he himself is a reflection of it in miniature, a
microcosm, possessing, and possessed and governed by, that
same divine reason which informs the whole universe.

This then is man's proper *areté* (is it not?), the excellence
which he alone among creatures can exercise; the disinterested
exercise of which, as Aristotle puts it, brings us as near to
godhead as we can get.

> Sure he that made us with such large discourse,
> Looking before and after, gave us not
> That capability and god-like reason
> To fust in us unus'd.

As the sun was setting, and the time was near for Socrates
to drink the hemlock, one of his friends, his last visitors in prison,
asked tearfully, 'How shall we bury you when it is over?' 'Any

way you like,' replied Socrates, 'if you can catch me.' 'I cannot convince Crito,' he complained to the rest of the company, 'that *this* is the real Socrates, who is conversing with you now.' Whatever it was that was choosing his words and marshalling his discourse, the *reasoner*, that was the real Socrates; not the stark, dumb husk which the poison would leave for his friends to dispose of.

Socrates's position is the opposite of Homer's, for whom the heroes' true selves were their bodies, not their souls which the anger of Achilles 'sent to the house of Hades, but themselves it made the prey of dogs and carrion birds'. Empedocles offered us the possibility (if we were prepared to follow his directions) of merging with our divine lodger or 'soul-mate', and so avoiding the fate of vanishing like smoke in the wind; Socrates not only saw all men as harbouring such a divine soul, but as themselves being linked with it, whether they liked it or not, so that the fortunes of the pair are inextricably conjoined; in other words, one's *self*-interest is identical with one's soul's interest.

'When you are gone, Socrates,' said Crito, 'how can we best act to please you?' 'Just follow my old recipe, my friend: do you yourselves concern yourselves with your own true self-interest; then you will oblige me, and mine, and yourselves too – whatever you may think of my present arguments. But if you neglect yourselves, and are not prepared to tread the path of life which I have mapped for you today and formerly, then however much you may profess agreement with me now you will in fact do me no very good turn.'

Real wisdom and enlightenment are to realise that the interest of our divine guest is paramount, and to seek to know what that interest is; for once it is known we shall inevitably act to further it, as it was a Greek axiom that no one knowingly acts against his own best interest. This is what is meant by the Socratic tenet that 'virtue is knowledge'; the way of salvation lies through intellectual illumination, not through purificatory ceremonies hawked about by magical ritualists.

These last provide matter for Socratic irony in Plato's account of his master's final hours, when an examination of the popular view of virtue (*areté*) reveals it as a sort of calculus of pleasures and pains: the just man is just because the pains of

right-dealing are counterbalanced for him by the prospect of
benefits to come, the temperate man is temperate from fear
of a hangover, and so on. Socrates voices an inkling that this
approach is all wrong.

Simmias, old friend, could it perhaps be that this is not
the currency in which true virtue trades – swapping
pleasures for pleasures and pains for pains, in higher or
lower denominations as if they were so much small change –
but that the true and golden standard, against which all these
other things should be measured and exchanged, is wisdom?
And if we have this yardstick within us, this wisdom, we
shall have a warranty of true fortitude and temperance and
right-doing, indeed of all real virtue, whether pleasures and
fears and suchlike are there in addition or not? But when
these last are bartered for each other in the absence of wisdom,
perhaps you have a mere silhouette of virtue, a cheat with
no health or truth in it, and the fact of the matter is that
your truly temperate and righteous and brave man is
cleansed of all such emotions, and that wisdom is his means of
attaining this cleansing. Perhaps the inventors of religious
services are not such rogues after all, when they threaten the
uninitiated with a mudbath in the next world, but promise
entrée to the circle of the gods for the cleansed initiate. As
you will remember, they are fond of saying that 'many profess
the god, but few possess him'. I think that maybe they are
hinting here, in a riddling way, at the few sincere cultivators
of wisdom.

These sincere cultivators of wisdom, these 'true philosophers',
will pursue goodness, truth and beauty, for these are acceptable
to the gods, whereas their opposites, the bad, the ugly and the
false, are totally foreign to them; and so, if we would be worthy
caretakers of our divine souls – our real selves – we will do
our best to give them the nourishment proper to deity, and
not to starve and stunt them with a rebarbative and stony diet.

But beauty, truth, goodness, what are these? By what criterion
shall we recognise them? Socrates's pupil Plato made ingenious
use of Pythagorean doctrine to answer this problem: Pythagoras
and Empedocles claimed lucid recollection, not only of their

previous incarnations, but of that heavenly homeland from which they had originally been banished. The generality of mankind, more obfuscated souls, have at best only dim half-memories of that blameless place, where we once knew the faces of perfect truth and perfect beauty and perfect goodness; but when our souls meet transient glimmerings of those faces in this world the half-memories are stirred and we feel a happy, lightsome urge to take off into the sky, or to procreate and recapture the moment of insight, either through the bodily instrument which we share with other life, or with the more esoteric instrument elaborated by the human mind – the creative, the poetic, techniques of the arts and crafts.

Uplift of the soul, its take-off into the sky: Plato would not have objected to the updating of these, his own, metaphors! As the individual person is thrust to birth by the imperative push of *thymos* and *philotimia*, he is also becoming conscious of a pull (which is represented or explicated artistically as a longing for a return to a lost state of godhood). Propelled into ever-growing selfconsciousness by those biological and social dictators, he begins to feel the attraction of another gravitational field. He is not circling back to his beginning, but spiralling into a new world, where free will will correspond to the necessity of chance in the world he is leaving.

4
Justice and Judgment

Hear the words of the hawk to the pretty nightingale, when he had grabbed her and carried her high into the clouds. She moaned pitifully as she was stabbed by the grip of his claws, but rough was his reply: 'You funny thing, why these shrieks? Your fate lies to be decided by one much your superior. Songstress you may be, but you will go where I take you – to free you if I wish, to eat you if I will.'

So the crusty Hesiod in the seventh century BC, telling 'a fable which will express their own thoughts' to the leading men of his native Ascra, who delivered judgments as cruel as the climate: for was it not their venality which had cheated Hesiod of his rightful inheritance? In so doing they had debased the very hall-mark of their humanity; they had crossed the frontier which marked them off from the beasts. 'Zeus, Kronos's son, has made this dispensation for men: that whereas fish and beast and feathered fowl devour each other, for they have no justice (diké) among them, he has given men diké, which is far the best thing.'

But Hesiod was living in the Age of Iron, and things had deteriorated sadly from the bliss of the distant Golden Age, when men lived the carefree life of the gods, without toil or tears, when earth lavished her bounty on them unasked, when the freshness of youth never left their limbs, and death finally stole upon them like sleep. But now Shame and Indignation were veiling their heads to depart back to heaven, and everywhere the protests of Justice could be heard as the quarrelsome moderns forced her to their whims. But she would go and crouch by the knees of her father Zeus, and bitterly denounce her ravishers to him and demand their punishment.

By Hesiod's time the concept of 'just-dealing' has so formed that it can be personified, into the maiden Justice; into what a

F   71

more sophisticated but duller age would call a 'principle of action'. Yet in the Homeric poems, not long before, this process has hardly begun. There, *diké* is basically the appropriate due, or the appropriate behaviour, prescribed by custom for persons falling into a certain class or performing a certain role; for instance, there is a proper form of burial according to the *diké* of mortals; to sleep comfortably is the *diké* of elders; the importunate and boorish rivals for the hand of Odysseus's Penelope do not woo her after the *diké* of suitors of former times.

So how I am expected to behave in given circumstances, and how you are expected to behave towards me, is determined by custom and by my, and your, social position. This is my *diké*, and the ability to recognise it separates men from brutes, just as to respect it separates civilised men from savages. Essentially, at this stage 'justice' is 'acting within one's own *diké*, and not encroaching on that of others'. But if such an encroachment should occur, or should be thought to have occurred, civilised men will not resort to force as a remedy, but to an arbiter or judge, who will define the *diké* of each of the disputants in the matter, decide whether the plaintiff's has suffered a diminution, and (if so) give judgment for its restitution; the defendant was then said to 'give *diké*' to the other.

Those best fitted to decide what the *diké* may be in a particular case will be those who have had most experience of past cases, and are the repositories of tradition – the elders of the community; and those whose decision of the case will be most acceptable will be those whose prestige, *timé*, is greatest – the nobles. They have a divine commission to safeguard the body of precedent, to decide appeals in accordance with it, and to hand it on to their successors.

In this state of affairs what *ought to be* is simply *what has been*; or rather, no explicit distinction is yet made between 'ought' and 'customarily is'. Absent is the assumption, which to us is a self-evident truth, that there is a criterion of 'justice' or 'rightness' which embraces, and may on occasion overrule, the criterion of tradition. To us, for instance, it is patently wrong, or unjust, that a man should arrogate to himself rule over others simply because his father had it before him. It would not occur to heroic society even to question such arrogation.

Yet this distinction, and the feeling that what *is* is not necessarily what *ought to be*, was even in those early days not far below the surface. It is there in Hesiod's regrets for the passing of the Golden Age; and it is there in the idea, expressed by a philosopher a century after Hesiod, that equality is a principle of nature's justice – that sharing equally is *right*.

This philosopher was Anaximander of Miletus, one of the first physical 'scientists', who saw the universe as composed of opposites – hot and cold, wet and dry, light and dark, and so on – which had emerged from the Indistinct or Unbounded. These opposites, he said, 'pay each other recompense (*diké* – 'render each other justice') for their aggression, in the sequence of time'. He had in mind the sequence of events throughout the year. At the temperate season of the vernal equinox day and night are equal in length. Then, as the summer gets hotter and drier, the hours of light encroach on those of darkness, diminishing them until the summer solstice, when day is longest and night shortest. Thenceforward, day gradually repays its thefts from the night, until at the autumnal equinox they are once more equal in length. But now the roles of assailant and victim are reversed: nights become longer at the expense of the days, until the climax of the winter solstice, when the process of repayment begins again, to last until the vernal equinox. It is a good example of man reflecting his social ideals on to his universe. Reciprocally, later (in Euripides) he would appeal to this principle of equality in nature to justify the principle of political equality in the state.

At first, custom needed no sanction beyond itself to ensure that it was respected; the prospect of social disapproval was enough to deter those who might have a mind to flout *diké*. But when men began to wink at the commission of injustice by others, and to feel no compunction at committing injustice themselves – when, as Hesiod put it, Shame and Indignation left the earth – what defence was left to the weak against the strong and unscrupulous and greedy?

What defence could there be, but Zeus himself? After all, it was he who had entrusted the laws to the safe-keeping of the nobles, and he might be expected to watch that his trust was not broken. So *diké*, the observation of customary due – that basic cement which bonded simple societies – was depicted by Hesiod as the daughter of Zeus, on whose paternal aid she can call in her distress.

The all-seeing eye of Zeus, observing even secret wrongdoers whom he would visit with condign punishment through the agency of his avenging Furies – all this was explained by a rational atheist of Socrates's day as the ingenious invention of some shrewd lawgiver of antiquity, to enforce by obscure super-natural terrors the continuing observance of co-operative behaviour by man, who is by nature anti-social and selfseeking. And no doubt there are modern sociologists who would find this explanation of these religious taboos acceptable enough, if one were to ascribe them, not to some imagined lawgiver of long ago, but to an 'inbuilt mechanism to reinforce socially useful behaviour'.

But the function of the lawgiver (or whatever we put in his place) would be simply to preserve that *diké* without which his little community would tear itself to pieces. Zeus however extended his shield further than this, to protect also the socially unproductive (beggars), outsiders in the society (visiting strangers), and contracts sealed by oath – which might be made between members of the same community, or (more interestingly) between different communities, who had no common *diké* to bind them. In the case of the helpless beggar or stranger, the hand of Zeus kept *force majeure* at bay; in the case of treaties between equally powerful communities, it secured what *force majeure* could not. It was, in other words, a civilising influence and presents a different aspect of Zeus from the philotimous god we have met, that projection of the historical ethos of heroic society. It is as if his vision of God spanned the sum of man's past and the trend of his future evolution – the rear of his retreating past and the vanguard of his approaching future – in a sort of 'specious present' of the soul.

Two or three miles from Oswestry, in the marches between England and Wales, on the road to Llanymynech (where there is an entrance to fairyland on the golfcourse), lies the hamlet of Llynclys, which name, being interpreted, signifieth 'the swallowed court'. Legend gives this account of it. Where the reeds now wave over Llynclys Pool there stood a fine palace, whither there once came the saint Germanus, or Garmon, preaching against the Pelagian heresy that Man can, unaided by divine grace, desire his own salvation. But the king would not listen to the saint's arguments; and so, in the depths of the night, when the king and his courtiers slept, the palace sank into the ground, and the waters silently rose about it; and even today you may, if you look hard and are very lucky, still discern beneath the surface the turrets of the building which was thus drowned with its occupants for their wicked stubbornness.

This story is a version, in Christian garb, of a very old and widespread folktale. Essentially, the story is of a footsore stranger (or pair of strangers) roughly refused hospitality by every house in the village save one. After the visitors' departure – who are in fact gods come in disguise to test men's humanity to each other – a neighbouring spring overflows miraculously, to drown all villagers except the hospitable ones. Perhaps the best-known version is (or used to be) that of Ovid in his *Metamorphoses*, told of Baucis and Philemon; but the germ of the story goes back seven centuries before Ovid, to the *Odyssey*, where some of the less overbearing of Penelope's suitors caution against the ill-usage of beggars on the ground that they may be gods *incogniti*:

> Antinous, you did not do well to strike this miserable vagabond. Now there will be trouble for us, if there is any god in heaven. For the gods take on all kinds of shapes, and go from city to city in the guise of foreigners, testing if the inhabitants are brutal or humane.

To these suitors, prudent men that they were, it was best to be on the safe side: the apparently helpless victim you were beating up might really be a god in disguise. What to Antinous's companions was only a possibility, to Empedocles and the Pythagoreans was to be a certainty: the unknown stranger, just as much as the known kinsman or neighbour, *is* a god, or carries a god within him, or is on his way to godhead – however you put it, the respect proper to a god is proper to him.

The punishment with which Zeus could be expected to visit an offender against his daughter *Diké* was the extirpation, not only of the guilty individual (perhaps not of him at all), but of his whole family. Initially it is the house, not the individual member of it, which has to bear the brunt of vengeance, and it is not yet felt that there is anything inequitable about this, when the family is still more 'real' than any individual member of it. 'Greatest and most glorious Zeus,' pray the Greeks and the Trojans as they ratify an inauspicious treaty with sacrifice and libations, 'and you other immortal gods: whichever side first violates this oath, may their brains spill upon the earth as this wine is now spilt, their and their children's brains, and may strangers have their wives.' It is a succinct prayer that the guilty stock be cut off root and branch.

With the broadening of political association into village and city (or city-state, *polis*), it is an easy step to envisage the whole community as suffering for the injustice of some member or members of it. In a simile in the *Iliad* rushing chariots are likened to rushing watercourses after a cloudburst:

> As when upon an autumn day the black earth feels the weight of the storm, when Zeus pelts it with rain in his anger at men who have given crooked judgments in court, snapped their fingers at the gods and run Justice (*Diké*) out of town: then the rivers brim, their banks tumble into the torrents which roar down headlong from the hills, and men's labours with the plough go to waste.

The whole community pays with the loss of its crops, with the loss of its livelihood, for its maladministration of justice.

The tone of this passage is very Hesiodic, and it is Hesiod who advises us most fully of the penalties for contempt, and the blessings for respect, of Justice which a society may expect.

> When men deal straight with townsman and stranger alike, and swerve not one whit from the path of justice, their city flourishes and their people bloom. Far-seeing Zeus decrees not for them the ruin of war, but peace throughout the land allows the youth to see manhood. No famine waits on men of straight judgment, nor destruction, but festive preparations are their portion. The earth showers them with cheer, for them the mountain oaks bear acorns on their branches and honey in their trunks, and the woolly sheep can hardly

support the weight of their fleeces. Their children are as good as the parents; nor must they import their livelihood in ships, but their own bountiful fields supply it all.

But from the lovers of impudence and aggressive mischief Zeus exacts requital; sure, one rotten member, one overbearing wrongdoer, can spread a blight through the whole community, on which heaven piles troubles. They die by hunger and they die by plague, and the populace dwindles; their women are barren and their households wither; or Zeus, Kronos's son, destroys their army, or throws down their walls, or sinks their ships. Such are his intentions for the unjust.

Not yet crystallised is the idea of the guilty individual, whose wilful act has produced unprofitable consequences, or whose mere act of will is deemed to be offensive in some way, and who therefore *himself* merits punishment. The misuse of personal responsibility does not yet incur a personal penalty in this world, let alone in any other, because the very idea of 'personal responsibility' is still inchoate.

Its formation might have been inhibited by the patent fact that the unjust, far from being punished, flourished like the green baytree; and this fact has indeed been adduced as a reason for the invention of hell, to the pains of which the losers in the philotimous race consigned the winners, thus awarding themselves a consolatory dish of sour grapes which can still set their descendants' teeth on edge. It is an alluring theory, but no less naïve than that of the 'lawgiver' to whose craftiness we were told we owe the invention of God.

Though the Titans, for their rebellion against Zeus, were imprisoned in Tartarus, a fearful place surrounded by bronze walls and threefold night, 'as far below the earth as the sky is above it', from which there is no escape, the Titans were gods of a kind. The Homeric House of Hades, the destination of all *human* dead, is no more depicted as a place of punishment than it is a place of reward. But to the most detailed account of it, the description of Odysseus's visit to consult the oracular dead, there is appended a passage (condemned even by ancient scholars as intrusive) about the tortures suffered by certain people in Hades: Tityos, fettered on his back while vultures tear at his liver, for he had ravished a paramour of Zeus; Tantalus, standing with water up to his chin and fruit dangling from branches just above his mouth, but always just out of his reach when he tries to assuage hunger or thirst (he had stolen ambrosia from the guest-table of Olympus, the food of the gods which confers immortality, and had shared it with his friends); and Sisyphus, the wily king who had tried to cheat the Lords of Death and return to the light of the sun and the living air, doomed to trundle a boulder to the top of a hill which he can never attain.

These lines, even if not original, could be quite early, for the toils of Sisyphus in the underworld were known to another poet writing about 600 BC. But even so it is noteworthy that the punishments are not inflicted for contraventions against *diké*, for breaches of a human code or custom; the victims are men who have offended in a very special way against the gods, setting themselves up as the gods' equals by forcing the beloved of Zeus or by trying to evade that main distinction between mortal and immortal – death.

In the *Iliad*, however, where Agamemnon swears an oath and, in ritual phraseology, calls woes down upon himself if he should swear falsely, the Furies are mentioned as punishing perjurers in hell:

> Be my witness and guard my oath, father Zeus, and thou Sun, who seest and hearest all; be my witness, rivers, and earth, and you who exact punishment of a dead man in the world below, if he has foresworn himself.

As these passages are anomalous, and as perjurers do not appear among the mortal sinners whom Odysseus saw suffering in the underworld, they were perhaps later insertions into the *Iliad*. There is an uncanny account of the punishment for oathbreaking in Hesiod, but the culprit here is not a man but a god.

In an almost inaccessible spot near the high summit of Mount Chelmos in southern Greece, the divine river Styx falls sheer over a line of beetling crags; fitting scenery for the emergence into daylight of the infernal river whose circling coils confine the subterranean dwelling of the dead. So potent and so magic were the waters of this hateful stream that the gods themselves

78

dared not take its name in vain. Hesiod gives the reason for this:

> When a quarrel starts among the immortals, and one of the
> dwellers on Olympus is lying, Zeus sends his messenger with
> a golden jug to fetch from afar some of that chill water for the
> gods to swear by, which pours over a lofty precipice; famous
> it is, a branch of Ocean's sacred stream, and most of it flows
> underground through the blackness of night. Nine-tenths of
> it wind to its mouth in silver eddies about earth and broad-
> backed sea; the remainder gushes from that steep, to the great
> sorrow of the gods. For if any of the immortal inhabitants of
> snowy Olympus defaults on his oath by the Styx, he lies
> with no breath in him for the space of a year. The sustenance
> of immortality, ambrosia and nectar, come not near his lips,
> but he sprawls on the coverlets of his bed neither speaking
> nor breathing, in the grip of an evil trance. And when, after
> the completion of a long year, his ailment has spent itself, a
> succession of labours awaits him, each one worse than the
> last. For nine years he is cut off from the company of the
> immortals, never joining their councils or their feasts; but
> in the tenth he is admitted once again to the assemblies of
> the Olympians.

The sufferer is a god; the sin for which he suffers is perjury;
and the punishment he suffers is an alteration of consciousness,
exclusion from the company of his divine peers, and a series of
unspecified but unpleasant 'labours', until he is finally restored
to his former state of blessedness. The Pythagorean Empedocles
clearly owed much to this Hesiodic passage in his description
of the divine soul, banished for the sin of perjury from the
company of the gods to suffer a succession of painful incarnations in earthly bodies before its final release and return home.

If the pains of hell were in fact an empty threat, invented to
ensure the observance of social justice by men, it is rather strange
that the first inkling of them concerns, not human contravention
of *diké*, but a god's default on his oath. But the enormity of the
sin, and the appropriateness of the punishment, are apparent if
the god's perjury is seen as deity *denying itself*. As far as I know,
this is a novel presentation of the matter; but, paradoxical though
it may be, let us keep it by us as a possibility for the moment.

The mystery religions, at least when we first hear of them, have no hell. The initiated souls, through their association with the god by the appropriate ritual, acquire an enhanced robustness and can share the joys of the divine company in the next life; the uninitiated, on the other hand, drag out a twilight existence in a limbo of boredom, but suffer no actual pains for their lack of initiation. It was the Pythagoreans who introduced into this scheme a dual refinement. First, the reward which the soul gets in the next world it earns, not by merely undergoing a ceremony, but by exhibiting certain moral qualities, in this one; secondly, *injustice* is regarded as a moral quality (or more accurately, an *im*moral one), and the unjust soul earns its own particular recompense in the world to come: sorrow instead of joy.

It was Pythagoras himself who introduced the former refinement; for his reputed master, Pherecydes, according to a poet of the fifth century BC, 'who excelled in manliness and modesty, even after death has an enjoyable life in the soul – if there is any truth in the teachings of Pythagoras, that cleverest of men'. Manliness and modesty were virtues in Homer's heroes too, but Pherecydes was no Homeric stalwart, and '*gentle*manliness' might here be the better translation of the Greek word. The important point is that it is because he exhibited these *moral* qualities that Pherecydes is thought of as enjoying himself in the next world.

If the divine soul could share the bliss of gods, it could share their pains too – and for the same reason. For the Pythagoreans held that we are as obliged to act rightly ('according to *diké*') as if we had sworn to do so: 'just-dealing has the force of an oath; this is why Zeus [the fountain-head and champion of Justice] is called the God of Oaths.' So the unjust soul, which spurns *Diké*, brings upon itself the penalties reserved for gods who break their oath, and there is a place in hell for the antisocial. *Diké*, the cement of the community, for the neglect of which it had been the community that suffered, is now armed with preternatural sanctions against the individual.

But, you may say, this scheme of reward or retribution in another world for actions done in this one is hardly compatible with that peculiarly Pythagorean doctrine of reincarnation, wherein this world itself is the scene of punishment for the soul which has sinned in its pristine state. True: the schemes are incompatible, they are not really complementary but duplicates, originating perhaps in an ambivalent view of man – is he a fallen god, or a god who may yet fall?

However, a combination of the two systems was contrived, after the following fashion. The errant soul is banished from heaven for a period of ten thousand years (each 'long year' of banishment suffered by Hesiod's perjured god is interpreted as a millennium). It begins each thousand-year period by being incarnated in an earthly body. After its separation from this at death it passes the balance of that period in receiving reward or punishment in a disembodied state for its deeds or misdeeds while in the flesh. It is then reincarnated, and the process is repeated until it finally escapes from the cycle – which may be before the completion of the full ten thousand years, for the consistently well-behaved.

A poetic description of this Pythagorean version of the fate of souls after death is given by Pindar, the elder contemporary of Empedocles:

> Equable the nights, equable the sun by day, labourless their livelihood for the good, who have no need to disturb earth or waters of the sea in the toil of their hands, in order to scrape a bare existence; but those to whom it was a joy to keep their oaths are allotted a life without tears in the fellowship of agreeable gods – while the others dree a weird not to be looked upon.
>
> And as many as have endured, through three sojourns on each side of the grave, to keep their souls quite from wrongdoing, to them Zeus reveals the road that leads to the tower of Kronos. There the ocean breezes play about the Island of the Blest, where globes of flowers gleam golden, some blossoming on land on noble trees, others in watery pastures, from which they twine garlands for their shoulders, guarded by the selfless concern of Rhadamanthys.

Here the haven to which the just souls escape from the cycle of rebirth is that rumoured Fortunate Isle, in search of which St Brendan set sail from an Irish harbour one evening some fourteen hundred summers ago, into the surge of the apple-green west. It is first heard of in Hesiod, who represents it as the dwelling of certain favoured heroes to whom Zeus granted immunity from death:

> Most of the men of the Heroic Age were enshrouded in death, but Zeus provided some with an estate to sustain them alive, settling them on the earth's edge, apart from men and apart from the Olympian gods, under the surveillance of his father Kronos. So they inhabit the Islands of the Blest by the deep eddies of Ocean, do these heroes, in carefree affluence, and the sweets of a bountiful soil crop for them thrice in every year.

But the most complete extant presentation in ancient literature of the combination of the idea of reincarnation with the idea of reward or punishment in the next world, between incarnations, for deeds done in this world, is in the story (or 'myth') of Er the Pamphylian, which is put into the mouth of Socrates by Plato in the tenth book of his *Republic* – the precursor of many a vision of the next world, both pagan and Christian. This Er was taken up among the dead after a battle, and his corpse was about to be cremated when it revived, and told the following tale.

'He said that, after he had departed out of his body, he found himself travelling with a great company, and they came to a mysterious place, where two openings in the earth next to each other faced two other openings in the heavens. Between these sat judges who, when they had judged the souls, despatched the righteous by the upper right-hand opening to heaven, first hanging on their breasts notices of the judgment, and the unrighteous by the downward path to the left; these also carried accounts of all their misdeeds, on their back. When Er approached, a voice told him that his task was to inform men of what happened here, and that he was ordered to observe and listen to all that passed in this place. Well, he saw souls departing by the entrances to heaven and earth aforesaid, when they had been judged, and souls ascending through the exit from the earth parched and filthy, while others descended through the heavenly exit spotless; and he heard each group inquiring of the other their experiences. And it was with groans and tears that the former recalled in their tale the sights and sufferings they had endured in their journey beneath the earth, but those from heaven told of joys and visions of miraculous beauty.

'To describe everything, Glaucon, would take too long; but the sum of the matter, as Er put it, was this: that for every wrong a man had done, and for every person he had wronged, he paid a tenfold penalty – for instance, if one had been responsible for the deaths of many of his fellowmen, or had helped to betray his country and its armies to enslavement or other maltreatment, for each he suffered tenfold pain; and the just and the righteous and the doers of good deeds were rewarded in like proportion.'

But emergence through the mouth leading from the subterranean road was not assured to everyone. 'Whenever one whose wickedness was incurable, or one who had not paid the penalty in full, tried to ascend, it would bellow. Then men of fierce and fiery aspect who were standing by, on hearing the sound, would seize some and drag them off; others they bound hand and foot, then flung them down and flayed them and, hauling them off to the side of the road, impaled them on spikes, and gave the other wayfarers to understand that those sinners were to be taken and cast into hell. Then, many and various as had been the terrors the souls had experienced on their way, this surpassed them all, each fearing lest the mouth should greet him with a bellow as he went up; and it was with the greatest relief that the ascent was accomplished in silence.'

The souls who had returned were now ready to be reborn into this world, and attended one of the Fates, Lachesis, for the allocation of their next life on earth.

'First, a herald ordered them in ranks, then taking lots and sketch-plans of lives from the lap of Lachesis he mounted a high platform and proclaimed: "Hear ye the decree of the maid Lachesis, the daughter of Necessity. Souls of a day, here begins for you another circle carrying the race of mortals to death. Your angel will not pick you, but you shall pick your angel. Let him who draws first place in the lot first choose the life to which he will be yoked by necessity. But Virtue owns no master: each will have more or less of her as he honours her more or less. The responsibility is on the chooser; there is none on God."

'With these words he flung the lots among the assembly, and each soul took the lot nearest to him, except Er, whom the herald forbade; and so each knew the order in which he should choose. Then the herald laid on the ground before them the life-plans – many more than there were souls present. These plans were of every sort, lives of every kind of beast and every kind of human. There were tyrannies among them, some carrying right through, some cut off short and ending in penury and exile and beggary; there were lives of men famous for physical beauty and bodily strength, or for noble birth and ancestral achievements, as there were too of men noted for none of these things; there were also lives of women. But there was no grading of soul, because soul would necessarily become different according to the life chosen.

'When the herald had spoken (Er said), the soul which had drawn first place came forward to choose, and chose to be the mightiest tyrant; but in its greedy haste it had not studied all that its choice involved, and had not noticed that among other ills it was to eat its own children; but when it examined its choice at leisure its lamentations were loud indeed, nor did it abide by the herald's warning; for it blamed not itself for its misfortunes, but its luck and the gods and everything rather than itself. Now this soul had been one which had come from heaven, having in its previous life lived in a constitutional democracy, where it had been virtuous by habit, without knowing why. Indeed, not the least part of those who fell into this trap were souls which had come from heaven, for they had not had the experience of harsh training; whereas those returning from beneath the earth, who had suffered themselves and seen others suffering, were in no hurry to make their choice. In this way most of the souls had an interchange of good and ill.

'And (Er said) it was a sight worth seeing, how each soul chose its next life; a sight to move one to pity, and laughter, and wonder. For they generally chose according to the lessons they thought they had learned from their past . . . And by chance he saw the soul of Odysseus, which had drawn the last place in the lottery, come forward to make its choice. It, remembering its former troubles and having had enough of prestige-seeking (*philotimia*), searched around and at length found in a corner the life of an obscure and retiring man, which the rest had brushed aside. When he saw it, he seized on it with alacrity, and said that he would have done the same even if he had had first choice.'

Is all this merely the product of poetic, or fevered, imagination? Or is it a hint of a spiritual transformation, a sign that Psyche had pioneered a new territory, and was moving into the possession of it; an inkling that, when 'to the just-pausing Genius we remit our worn-out life', we may not simply become 'what we have been'? Or not at once? Or not in every case? Let us turn aside and ruminate a little on the matter, for the issue may not be without importance.

On a hot summer's day in 1838, when the Reverend S. Baring-Gould was four years of age, he was seated on the box of a carriage as it passed through a bleak and arid plain in the south of France. Suddenly he was surprised to see a host of dwarfs scampering alongside the equipage, scrambling on to the horses' backs, and sitting laughing on the pole. When he remarked on this to his father, the child was promptly put inside the coach, and the merry little fellows gradually disappeared from his sight. Years later his own son, then about twelve, was in the garden picking peas for the cook, when he was terrified to come upon a little man standing between the rows, in a red cap, green jacket and brown breeches, 'whose face was old and wan, and who had a grey beard and eyes as black and hard as sloes'. Baring-Gould's wife, too, when a girl of fifteen, was startled by the sight of a little green man, a foot or so high, staring at her with beady black eyes from a privet hedge.

One should not be overnice in classifying such apparitions, but the scientifically-minded might be inclined to group them with what Robert Burton calls 'terrestrial devils' – 'those lares, genii, fauns, satyrs, wood-nymphs, foliots, fairies, Robin Good-fellows, *trolli*', which 'dance on heaths and greens, as Lavater thinks with Trithemius, and, as Olaus Magnus adds, leave that green circle, which we commonly find in plain fields', and 'are sometimes seen by old women and children'.

Baring-Gould thought that it was all caused by the action of the sun's heat upon the head – as I suppose it might have been also in the case of the little Yorkshire girl who came in from the garden one summer evening to find the parlour full of what she called 'addlers and menters', one of whom, a small man wearing a green coat and a gold-laced cocked hat, tried to get her to dance with him. To be more precise: Baring-Gould thought that the sun's heat was what Aristotle would have called the *efficient* cause – it triggered the hallucination – but the content of the hallucination, the size and dress and behaviour of the figures seen, was shaped by the expectations of the percipients; they saw, in a place where they expected, or half-expected, to see them, beings looking and behaving as their seers had been led, from written descriptions or artistic illustrations, to suppose such beings would do (Aristotle's *formal* cause).

When the Assyrian Esarhaddon's troops, marching through the desert of Sinai, saw two-headed serpents and green monsters with wings, we may readily allow the efficient cause to have been heat and exhaustion. Such a combination may have played its part also in the vision of Pheidippides in 490 BC. He ran a hundred and fifty miles in two days, between Athens and Sparta, and while doing so was intercepted by the god Pan on the wild Mount Parthenius on the border of Arcadia and the Argolid (where I had a puncture in 1962), who reproached the Athenians with their neglect of his worship. To debate the formal cause in this case would be fruitless, as Pheidippides has left us no description of Pan as he appeared to be; but what seems to be a fine example of a hallucination shaped by artistic representation is the appearance of the goddess Athena in panoply by the bedside of Aelius Aristeides in the second century AD. She was of a beauty and stature more than human – like the statue of her by Pheidias in the Parthenon, in fact – and was invisible to the friends of Aristeides, who was in the grip of the plague at the time. This is reminiscent of the vision of Benvenuto Cellini, who, in the crisis of a near-fatal fever in 1535, was approached by a terrible old man who tried to throw him into a huge boat. 'Messer Lodovico asked me who it was I saw, and what he was like. While I was drawing his picture exactly in words, the old man took hold of my arm and hauled me forcibly towards him, so that I called out to them to help me, for he was going to throw me down to the bottom of his fearsome boat.' And thrown into the boat Cellini seemed to himself to be, and appeared to his friends to be dead. What he saw was Charon, the aged and unkempt demon 'with fire staring from his eyes', who ferried the souls of the dead across the infernal river Styx – as he was described by Virgil and Dante.

Such hallucinations, then, may owe their occurrence to certain abnormal physical conditions in the percipient, and their form to artistic representations known to him (whether verbal or plastic). They may also require a belief, either of the percipient or generally of his community, that such representations correspond to reality. That community beliefs may play an important part in an individual's hallucinations is an interesting suggestion of G. N. M. Tyrrell:

It seems as if the more incoherent types of haunting were due to idea-patterns only very loosely connected, or perhaps not connected at all, with any idea in a conscious mind. One wonders whether such subconsciously initiated idea-patterns may in some cases be collective. If they were, they would throw light on many age-old traditions and legends. Popular tradition might supply material out of which such collective idea-patterns could be formed. Take, for example, the idea of the god Pan, half human and half goat-like, haunting certain places in the woods and uplands and playing his pipe. The widely spread idea that this happened might conceivably sink into the mid-levels of the personalities of a whole community, and there form a telepathic idea-pattern, having a multiple agency. Anyone (suitably sensitive) going to the places which, according to the idea-pattern, Pan was especially supposed to inhabit would then see and hear Pan with exactly the same reality that a person going into a haunted house sees and hears a ghost.

I find the theory an attractive one. It would explain the nymph, or 'semblance of a female figure draped in white and tall beyond human stature', which John Lawson and his guide once saw 'flitting in the dusk between the gnarled and twisted boles of an old olive-yard' on a Greek mountainside. It might also explain why, when I used to hunt for a glimpse of Pan in the north Welsh woods, among the hedge-garlic and the oaks stunted by the westerlies of many an equinox, I never saw him: he was not an 'idea-pattern' of the Welsh community!

Perhaps Pan is no longer an 'idea-pattern' even in Greece. On the other hand, in the Second World War a British soldier was passing a night on the Aegean island of Cos, once the home of Hippocrates, called 'the father of medicine'. His billet was a solitary spot beneath the stars, with no sign of human habitation save the stubs of some ancient pillars and a long stone slab in the midst of them. He fell into an uneasy sleep, in which his dreams were haunted by the presence of a youngish, bearded man in an outlandish smock. The experience had an unusual quality about it, and later he learned that he had been in the ruins of the temple of Asclepius, the Greek god of healing, where the sick used to come to sleep in the hope of a nocturnal visitation and therapy by the god (the practice called incubation). The dream figure was remarkably like ancient statues of Asclepius, any previous knowledge of whom, however, this dreamer disclaimed. Whether the Coans still have an 'idea-pattern' of the god their ancestors consulted, I do not know; but incubation for the cure of disease has been practised even in modern times in nearby islands, and indeed in Greece generally.

It seems likely that waking hallucinations are of the same order as sleeping ones, dreams. Normally, the actors and properties in one's dreams are reflections, even if distorted and recombined, of people and things one has known in everyday life. But an interesting hint that the forms of art may also invade a man's dreams is given by Dr. van Eeden, who, discovering that he quite frequently had an odd type of dream, in which he *realised* he was dreaming (these he called 'lucid dreams'), between 1898 and 1913 recorded about five hundred of his dreams. In his records there featured a kind of 'non-lucid' dream often enough for him to give it a name. The name he gave it was 'demon dream', because the actors were very like medieval artists' depictions of devils.

In such dreams these beings, fluid in form and sex, would surround him, mock him, and try to engage him in scenes of horror or obscenity. C. D. Broad quotes a typical example:

Immediately, after a succession of very beautiful lucid

dreams, a demon dream began. Van Eeden found himself as it were surrounded by a number of these creatures. They started singing, like a mob of half-savage beings. In the dream he began to lose self-control, and, as it seemed, started throwing his bed-clothes and pillows about. At this point he noticed one of the demons, who looked less vicious than the rest. This one said to him: 'You are going wrong!' Van Eeden answered: 'Yes, but what shall I do?' The demon . . . answered: 'Give them the whip on their naked backs!' Thereupon van Eeden, thinking of a relevant passage in Dante, proceeded to 'materialise' a whip of leathern thongs with leaden balls at the ends of them. He threatened the demons with this, whereupon they slunk away.

There is more than one link here with the Tibetan *Book of the Dead*. This work may be described as a science of dying, of the *psychochemistry* of physical dissolution, a guide and handbook for the journey all must make. However, it falls far short of the rigorous standards of western science, inasmuch as its propositions cannot be tested publicly in a laboratory, but only privately and when the opportunity to publish the experience is generally supposed to have passed. Even so, it may deserve the name of science insofar as it implies the power of the acolyte, if he has mastered it, to control his environment.

It purports to tell the newly-dead man about the 'forty-nine days' he is now to endure in the Bardo, the state 'between existences', to warn him of the dangers that lurk there, and to instruct him how to comport himself in the face of them. Into the ear of the corpse, or of a dummy representing the dead man, the minister and mentor mutters his words of guidance, explaining to the lonely wanderer what he is to expect at each stage of his way, exhorting and instructing him how to react for the best. The supreme aim will be for the dead one to escape from the cycle of rebirth, perpetual individuation. This goal may be attained at any point in the Bardo, but is more or less impeded by the accumulated 'resonance' of the man's behaviour in his lifetime (*karma*); which operates more and more irresistibly as (and if) he reaches the later and more terrifying stages of the Bardo, when his past will be sweeping him like a great wind, perhaps back into the human world, or into the brute world, or into hell. Liberation occurs if at any point he realises that the visions which now fill him with panic are self-induced hallucinations, various reflections of the good which he shunned in life; and if with this realisation the terror is replaced by a love for, and longing to be merged with, this good.

O nobly-born, when such thought-forms emanate, be thou not afraid, not terrified; the body which thou now possessest being a mental body of *karmic* propensities, though slain and chopped to bits, cannot die. Because thy body is, in reality, one of voidness, thou needest not fear. The bodies of the Lord of Death, too, are emanations from the radiances of thine own intellect; they are not constituted of matter; voidness cannot injure voidness. Beyond the emanations of thine own intellectual faculties, externally, the Peaceful and Wrathful Ones, the rainbow lights, the terrifying forms of the Lord of Death, exist not in reality: of this, there is no doubt. Thus, knowing this, all the fear and terror is self-dissipated; and, merging in the state of at-one-ment, Buddhahood is obtained. If thou recognisest in that manner, exerting thy faith and affection towards the tutelary deities and believing that they have come to receive thee amidst the ambuscades of the Bardo, think, 'I take refuge in them'.

The hallucinations described in the Tibetan *Book of the Dead* model themselves, not unnaturally, on the iconography of Tantra Buddhism. Those who have other religious beliefs will experience other forms; and those who have none, presumably nothing.

One day in 1854 George Borrow, dry and dusty with foot-slogging through the bounds of Eryri, turned into the inn at Tan-y-bwlch. He found the bar-parlour occupied by a solitary morose stranger, refreshing himself with 'a glass of something'. They soon got into conversation, and the conversation soon took a religious turn, about whether man was foredoomed and God foreknew. 'He asked me whether I hoped to be saved; I told him I did, and I asked him whether he hoped to be saved. He told me he did not, and as he said so, he tapped with a silver tea-spoon on the rim of his glass. I said that he seemed to take very coolly the prospect of damnation; he replied that it was of no use taking what was inevitable otherwise than coolly. I asked him on what ground he imagined he should be lost; he replied, on the ground of being predestined to be lost. I asked him how he knew he was predestined to be lost; whereupon he asked me how I knew I was to be saved. I told him I did not know I was to be saved, but trusted I should be so by belief in Christ . . . At last, finding him silent, and having finished my brandy-and-water, I got up, rang the bell, paid for what I had had, and left him looking very miserable, perhaps at finding that he was not quite so certain of eternal damnation as he had hitherto supposed.'

Borrow surmised that preoccupation with their own damnation gives some folk a sort of perverted self-importance: they must, they feel, be something particular, or God would not trouble himself to torment them for ever. Such a diagnosis would doubtless have infuriated Samuel Johnson, who passed many a sleepless night agonising over the possibility that he was lost, that on the Day of Judgment he would hear those terrible words addressed to him, 'I know you not'; and he often kept Mrs. Thrale up till all hours drinking tea, to postpone the time of bed and self-recrimination. 'As I cannot be *sure* that I have fulfilled the conditions on which salvation is granted,' he told Dr. Adams, 'I am afraid I may be one of those who shall be damned.' His companion asked him what he meant by 'damned'. 'Sent to hell, Sir,' shouted Johnson, 'and punished everlastingly.'

Johnson had a literal mind, with little time for metaphysical subtleties, as is witnessed by that famous occasion when he refuted Bishop Berkeley's theory that our physical world is an idea in the mind of God, by kicking a stone so that his foot rebounded from it. To be sent to hell implies a place to be sent to, though I do not know that Boswell ever asked him if he subscribed to the view, held by some earlier authorities, that 'there be certain mouths of hell, and places appointed for the punishment of men's souls, as at Hecla in Iceland, where the ghosts of men are familiarly seen, and sometimes talk with the living'; likewise 'those sulphureous vulcanian islands' of Lipari etc., Tierra del Fuego, 'those frequent volcanoes in America and that fearful mount Hecklebirg in Norway, "where lamentable screeches and howlings are continually heard, which strike a terror to the auditors; fiery chariots are commonly seen to bring in the souls of men in the likeness of crows, and devils ordinarily go in and out".'

There were those who argued that hell could not be within the earth, because there would not be room enough there; but the mathematical Lessius opined that this local hell need be no more than one Dutch mile in diameter to accommodate 800,000 millions of damned souls, allowing each soul six cubic feet – which Lessius thought amply sufficient, as unquestionably the sum of all the damned will not exceed 100,000 million.

I do not know on what evidence Lessius based his optimistic projection of the complete number of the non-elect. It could hardly have been the testimony of that lost soul which was permitted to return briefly to earth only a few days after its death, and was amazed to find anyone left here. The fall of souls into hell was like a perpetual snowstorm. Indeed, in the later Middle Ages the ordinary man's chance of escaping hell was reckoned as practically zero, and the ordinary woman's as less.

However, there need be no housing problem if we accept the assurance of Marlowe's Mephistophilis, that

> Hell hath no limits, nor is circumscribed
> In one self place; for where we are is hell,
> And where hell is, there must we ever be.

In 1962 H. H. Price, some time Wykeham Professor of Logic in the University of Oxford, addressed the Society for Psychical Research on the subject of 'Survival and the Idea of "Another World".' Here his concern was not to examine evidence for or against the existence of 'another world', but to rebut those who hold that the very idea of life after death is unintelligible; that the hypothesis of personal survival is a meaningless hypothesis; and that there is no point in speculating about a world other than the physical world we know.

Price meets these objections by suggestion that 'the Next World, if there is one, might be a world of mental images. Nor need such a world be so thin and insubstantial as you might think. Paradoxical as it may sound, there is nothing imaginary

about a mental image. It is an actual entity, as real as anything can be . . . Indeed, to those who experienced it an image-
world would be just as "real" as this present world is; and perhaps so like it that they would have considerable difficulty in
realising that they are dead . . . There might be a set of visual
images related to each other perspectivally, with front views
and side views and back views all fitting neatly together in
the way that ordinary visual appearances do now.' Images of
smell and touch might be added, to form 'families of images',
which might be grouped together to make 'a perfectly good
world'. Price sees no difficulty in the idea that such a world
of mental images might be experienced by a disembodied person;
that the experience of *feeling alive* 'could occur in the absence of
a physical organism', that 'a disembodied personality could *be*
alive in the psychological sense, even though by definition it
would not be alive in the physiological or biochemical sense'.

Clearly such a world would not be *in* physical space at all,
and 'passing' to it from the physical world should be thought
of as a change of consciousness, analogous to passing from a
waking to a dreaming state. And just as such a world would
not be in physical space, so there might be any number of
them—just as many as those who experienced them, in fact:
quot homines, tot mundi. And the material of which they would
be formed (if I may put it so) would be the memories and
desires of their inhabitants – or rather inhabitant, for there would
be only one to each, and he would be a sort of god in it, monarch
of all he surveyed. But it would be a barren world, in the sense
that its only other occupants would be puppets created by his
own imagination, self-limited and incapable of fertilisation from
outside. 'His world would be, so to speak, the outgrowth of
his character; it would be his own character represented to him
in the form of dream-like images. There is therefore a sense in
which he gets exactly the sort of world he wants', yet what he
really wants may not be clear even to himself, and the conflict
may be presented to him in fearful forms. 'To use scriptural
language, the secrets of his heart will be revealed – at any rate
to himself. These formerly repressed desires will manifest themselves by appropriate images, and these images might be
exceedingly horrifying . . . True enough, they will be "wish-

fulfilment" images . . . but the wishes they fulfil will conflict with other wishes which he also has. And the emotional state which results might be worse than the worst nightmare; worse, because the dreamer cannot wake up from it.' Each one of us can look forward to being his own judge and executioner; and what could be fairer?

As I have said, in this lecture Price was not concerned to examine evidence that an 'after-death state' has in fact ever been experienced. But this was done monumentally by another philosopher, Professor C. D. Broad of Cambridge University, whose *Lectures on Psychical Research* were published in 1962. To this I refer the interested reader, who will find therein much food for thought. Professor Broad in his preface confesses to a personal predilection for annihilation:

> If there should be another life, one can judge of its possibilities only by analogy with the actualities of life on earth. Nothing that I know of the lives and circumstances of most human beings in the present and past encourages me to wish to risk encountering similar possibilities after death. If death be the end, one knows the worst; and the worst, if it ceases to be bearable, is at any rate evitable. If death be not the end, then one is confined for all sempiternity in what looks unpleasantly like a prison or a lunatic-asylum, from which there is in principle no escape.

If Professor Price's hypothesis about the nature of the next world is right, Professor Broad need not worry. Anyway, over the page he quotes Mr. Wackford Squeers on Nature: 'She's a rum 'un is Natur'. Natur' is more easier conceived than described.' And it was, I think, yet another professor, the biochemist J. B.S. Haldane, who warned us that our universe may not only be a more mysterious place than we imagine, but a more mysterious place than we *can* imagine.

Parallel with the extrapolation, during these formative centuries, of the political individual from his social roles, the proliferation of the 'heroic self', there was also emerging from the idea of a vital principle (*psyché*) the idea of a morally responsible *soul*, capable of deciding its own preternatural destiny. The heroic self, driven by *thymos*, steered by *philotimia*, is *braked* by *diké*, respect for dues which have been established by the tradition of its society. Its controller – social tradition – though acknowledged by itself, is yet external to itself. The morally responsible soul, on the other hand, is self-controlled – by its own freely-given word, its *oath*. A link was forged between the supra-political, other-worldly, self (the soul) and the political, or worldly, self, by the idea that acting justly towards others, acting according to *diké* ('right-working'), has the obligatory force of an oath. This offered the possibility of orderly change when social traditions began to break down with the proliferation of 'heroic selves'.

The concept of *diké* was changing and deepening: it was no longer simply knowledge of, and respect for, traditional dues; the feeling was growing that established custom is not necessarily what *ought* to be. The change is reflected in the appearance of a sense of equity, a sense that what is just (in the narrow interpretation) may yet not be *fair*.

Plato was much exercised to discover the nature of this subtler *diké*, to know how men ought to behave in communities; and his longest work, the *Republic*, is devoted to investigating what 'just-dealing', or 'right-working', exactly is.

As I have said, *diké* was the restraint, or brake, on *philotimia*, and we have already met what might be called the ideal philotimous man, Callicles, putting it forcibly to Plato's master Socrates that this restraint is unnatural, a mere confidence trick devised by the weak in their own protection, to cheat the strong out of the takings that could be theirs. The strong man is bemused into foregoing the power and pleasures which are his to hand, in exchange for the empty esteem of the weakling majority for this phantom 'justice'. How, if at all, can Callicles be answered?

Early in the *Republic* Socrates is faced squarely with the problem by his young friends Glaucon and Adeimantus (Plato's brothers). Glaucon acts as 'devil's advocate' for what he calls the popular view of just and unjust dealing.

According to this view, he says, just dealing is a 'good' only in the sense that gymnastic exercise or medical treatment is 'good': undesirable in themselves, men yet put up with their unpleasantness for the sake of their consequences. 'Men say that by nature to prey on others is good, to be preyed on by others is bad, but that we suffer more harm as prey than we gain benefit as predators; so, when men do wrong and suffer wrong and know the taste of both, as they cannot escape the latter and get away with the former they decide that it would pay to agree with one another to do neither.' Out of this 'social contract' or compromise between the best (doing injustice with impunity) and the worst (having to suffer it without remedy) come laws and *diké*. This 'justice' is generally praised, not for its own sake, but because of its social utility; no one in his right mind, if he had the power to inflict wrong with impunity, would enter into such a contract.

Glaucon drives home his point with a couple of hypotheses. Imagine, he says, your reputedly just man as being freed from all fear of the consequences of his actions – confer on him the power of becoming invisible at will, for instance. Then his behaviour would be exactly like that of the unjust man, for he would be led on by 'the desire to get more for himself, which it is in the essence of every nature to aim after as good, though law has trained and bent us to value equality'. Or let us set a portrait of the ideally just man alongside one of the ideally unjust man, and see which is the more choiceworthy.

'To the perfectly unjust man we must allow perfect injustice without detracting one jot from it: we must let him win the greatest reputation for righteousness while committing the greatest wickedness. If ever he makes a mistake he must be able to retrieve it, and he must be a good enough talker to talk his way out if he is ever denounced for his wrongdoing; and where force is needed he must be able to use it, through his own physical strength and bravery backed up by wealth and friends. Having postulated him to be such, let us imagine beside him our just man, a simple and decent fellow who wants (as Aeschylus puts it) "to be good not in name but in truth". Very well, let us start by stripping him of the name; for if he is seen to be righteous the semblance will win him rewards and honours, and it will not be clear whether he is righteous for righteousness's sake or for the sake of the rewards and honours.

'Let him then, though he has never wronged anyone, have the reputation of the very worst wrongdoer, and let him bear this reputation unalloyed till his death, always acting justly throughout his life while being accused of every injustice. Then, when our two paragons have each exemplified perfection in his own way, the one of justice, the other of injustice, let the verdict be given which of them is the happier.' The perfectly unjust man will win political power and riches, by means of which he will be able to help his friends and harm his enemies, yes, and honour the gods too as they should be honoured, with magnificent offerings. Thus he will have the favours of men and of heaven. What a contrast to the fate in store for our ideally just man, who will be 'scourged, racked, fettered, have his eyes burnt out, and finally be impaled, and will realise that a man ought to want, not to be, but to seem to be, righteous'.

Adeimantus echoes his brother's contention, that it is the image of righteousness rather than the reality which men prize, and the attendant benefits rather than the virtue itself. 'Of all you who profess to be admirers of justice, from the earliest heroes whose words have been bequeathed to us to the present day, no one has ever condemned wrong-doing or praised right-doing except in terms of the honours and benefits, material and immaterial, which they bring. No one has ever told us the hidden power with which it acts on the soul of its possessor, and demonstrated to us that acting unjustly is of all the soul's capabilities the greatest evil, and acting justly the greatest good. But if you had all directed your teaching to this end, if you had brought us up from childhood to see this, we would not now all be watching our neighbour to stop him doing wrong, but we would each be watching himself (and what better watchdog could there be?), to ensure that he did not, by acting unjustly, find himself in the company of the greatest evil.'

Socrates meets the challenge by evolving, in the course of a lengthy debate, a theory of 'justice' which uses a sense of the Greek word that I have tried to get by the rendering 'right-working' – an ambiguous phrase, which can mean 'acting righteously (or justly)' or 'functioning correctly'. We would not apply the term 'just' to a motor vehicle, all of whose parts were functioning perfectly, but a Greek of Socrates's time could have done so. So, 'just' is an adjective which is applicable to a whole with subordinate parts, or to any combination for a purpose: 'justice' in the body is the correct functioning of the various parts of the whole organism (what is usually called 'health'); 'justice' in the state is the correct functioning of all the classes within it; 'justice' in the individual is the correct functioning of the parts of his soul in relation to each other (what I suppose would today be called 'integration of the personality'). On this view, then, 'justice' (or 'right-working') can be described as the health of the soul – the desirability of which is as self-evident as the health of the body, and needs no special pleading.

Socrates (or his reporter Plato) is here using the principle of *harmony*, which the Pythagoreans saw as underlying the working of the whole universe, and is applying it to lesser 'wholes'. Justice 'does not concern a man's dealings with others but with himself: it is really about himself and his relation with himself, when he does not allow any one of the parts of his soul to overstep its own sphere and to interfere with the others, but puts his own house in order in the truest sense of the phrase, governs himself, marshals himself, befriends himself, and harmonises those three elements within him, just like three notes in a musical scale, binding them together so that what had been many becomes one, sane and harmonious (*or* self-consistent)'. (The 'elements' of the soul, here referred to, Plato postulated to be three – the sensual or libidinous, the passionate or impulsive, and the rational; in the 'just' soul the last controls the two former.) It is better 'to be out of tune with the rest of the world than to be out of tune with one's self, who should be a unity'. The discordant soul suffers the disasters that attend civil war. A family or state divided against itself will perish, and, if he is to *persist*, even Satan must be self-consistent.

To define justice as 'the health of the soul' is, however, descriptive rather than prescriptive: it does not tell us what right action is, but how we may know if we have acted rightly. It is no more a guide to action than if a doctor were merely to tell his patient, 'Be healthy!'

Plato has produced a most interesting thesis: that there is such a thing as mental (or 'spiritual') health as well as bodily health, which is enjoyed by the just but not by the unjust – that virtue is indeed its own reward, for flouting the rules of spiritual hygiene automatically brings its own punishment, as naturally as does flouting the rules of physical hygiene. Indeed (if the story of Er's vision of the next world is anything more than an artistic climax to the book), it is more important to preserve this spiritual health than that of the body, for its effects are deeper and last longer.

Yet even Plato's 'justice' lacks sinew. It has not the positive power to move men to action, as has *philotimia;* not surprisingly, if *diké* was originally negative, the restraint or brake on *philotimia.* In the world of the philotimous 'heroic self' justice plays a necessary role, though a negative one, for without it society would break down. For the 'anti-hero', the individual self extruded by philotimous society but set outside and over against it, *diké* could have no power at all – least of all as a spring of action that would replace that *philotimia* which had been abandoned.

5

The New Man

When Er, in his vision of the next world, saw the souls who were about to embark on another 'circle that carries the mortal race to death' choosing the pattern of their new life on earth, he noted that among the options there was no determination of soul, 'because, of necessity, the soul becomes different according as it chooses a different life'. Plato is saying that the soul is a free, self-determining agent – 'the responsibility is on the chooser. There is none on God' – for him, and for Socrates, the soul is the 'moral self', and indeed the true man.

This subtle and elevated view of *psyché* would not have commended itself to the generality of Plato's contemporaries, and the use of the word in this sense is open to objections. But what other word to use for this new vehicle of experience which had come into being like a chemical fusion in a biological and social process? Though of course the Greeks and Romans knew the self as a reflexive pronoun (one could 'help one's self', 'kill one's self', even 'know one's self', and so on, in Greek and Latin), they did not substantiate it as a noun.

Yet as the 'physical self' and the 'social self' already preceded the complex fusion of the 'moral self' – the hybrid 'child of earth and starry heaven', hankering after some dimly apprehended state of blessedness – another term was really needed for the new entity. One might be culled from a strange passage in the *Odyssey*, when Odysseus visited the ghosts on the twilight fringes of the earth. Among them he saw the grim figure of Heracles, 'lowering like night, with bow bared and an arrow on the string, peering fiercely this way and that, as if looking for a target', and all about him the shades of the dead squeaked in terror as they tumbled to get out of his way; only it was not Heracles but an image (*eidolon*) of him, 'for he himself is on Olympus with the immortal gods, where he shares their feasts and the bed of Hebe of the slim ankles'. Essentially, the new man who was making his debut in the world was not so much a *psyché* as an *eidolon*, a phantom reflection of something whose animating principle (*psyché*) is elsewhere. Well, anyway let us temporarily stop this 'soul-ache' (or whatever it is that makes people deplore what some call 'the human situation') by positing the appearance of such *psychic eidola* here and there, and now and then (who would number or place them?), in classical Greece.

But perhaps it is old fashioned, and even obscurantist, to postulate the birth of new vehicles of experience, and to substantiate or particularise what would more acceptably be described now as a *process* of cultural evolution. Maybe so; but what is out of fashion today may be in fashion tomorrow, and in this chapter I want to remark on certain phenomena, which can be seen as mere features of cultural change in the classical world in the last six centuries before Christ, or as glimpses of an infantile *eidolon* of a new man, not better so much as faddier than his forebears; one whose spiritual appetite was not to be satisfied with the old diet.

The trend of the times, towards a sense of the distinctness of one individual from all others and an interest in the differing characteristics of individuals, has been noticed by many scholars. One, D. R. Stuart, has summed it up well:

> In the fourth century life in the mass and life in the individual came to be an engrossing concern . . . The Greek citizen was finding himself more of a personal entity than he had been in earlier times . . . The average life was no longer a bubble borne onward in the flow of the main current but one that might circle in eddies apart.

Sculpture particularly well illustrates the changing attitude to individuality:

> The portrait sculpture of the fifth century deals in types in which the variety of specific likeness is mostly lost in idealization. In the fourth century verisimilitude prevails in delineation of the human subject; a god as well becomes under the hands of Praxiteles a creature susceptible to mood and with an aspect of human charm.

Indeed, the beginning of the process can already be seen in the plastic art of the mid-fifth century, where archaic stylisation is starting to yield to naturalism, but naturalism elevated and dignified. The change has been explained as simply a reflection of technical advance: the artist has not changed, but his tools have. It looks like the old problem of which came first, the hen or the egg. 'Still,' wrote Nesca Robb when discussing a very similar change in the art of the Italian Renaissance, 'with any genuine artist technical developments do not take place entirely *in vacuo*; they are always in some measure the result of an inward movement. The means of expression grow and change because there are new ideas to be expressed; and through the exercise of art fresh ideas are brought into being.' This is the essence of cultural 'feedback', *psychopoeia* or *soulmaking*.

Stuart continues:

No wonder then, with . . . the greater distinctness of the individual in the scheme of things, and the competence given by ethics to estimate personal worth and conduct, that literature responded by extending and refining that sculpturing of personality in the round which the prose encomium had already begun. Formal biography was the finished product.

The lives and activities of personages who had lived in the recent past were becoming objects of interest, in addition to the deeds of legendary heroes, whose existence was not questioned but whose historicity seemed somehow to be beyond denial or affirmation, as if it had had its place in an order of time and space slightly different from our own. Now, realisation was dawning that *history* is edifying, and that history is shaped by individuals.

Yet these edifying individuals were initially important personages in the state, the leaders, who approached heroic status. 'John Smith' had to wait for Stephen Leacock to find a biographer; but John Smith too was edging into the limelight (though that epic of nonentities, the novel, was still a long way off).

In the *Iliad* 'John Smith', the private infantryman in the Greek or Trojan army, was lost in an undifferentiated, anonymous mass. He was there to acclaim his captains' decisions, and to provide them with sword-fodder (Patroclus slaughtered twenty-seven John Smiths with three leaps into the enemy ranks). The only commoner portrayed in the poem, the loud-mouthed Thersites who was always nagging his betters, is cruelly rendered: lame, round-shouldered, with a bald misshapen head, a scarecrow rather than a man, he was 'the most disgusting member of the whole expeditionary force against Troy' (the Greek word here translated as 'disgusting' includes ugliness both of body and of character). It is true that in the *Odyssey* an important part is played by Odysseus's faithful swineherd Eumaeus, who is treated at length and with sympathy; but he turns out to have been born an aristocrat, a king's son kidnapped in infancy and sold abroad into slavery by knavish Phoenician merchants.

One might suppose that it was in comedy that the common man first came to occupy the centre of the stage. But the operation of comedy was peculiar: it worked not to elevate the individual but to reduce all individuals, whoever they were, to sameness; to remind us – as it was put to me (not in so many words) by a fellow-soldier in 1940 – that however nicely adventitious embellishments distinguished officers from men on the parade ground, in the privy we all rank equal. It is in tragedy that lowly people – a peasant, a sentry, a servant – are presented with a touch which gives them a being of their own. They often have a slightly comic flavour, but the nurse in Euripides's *Hippolytus* plays a crucial role, and in his *Electra* the farmer to whom the princess Electra has been married by her scheming stepfather is a man of quite exceptional chivalry (the poet does give him some 'blue blood', but this is doubtless a concession to the feelings of the audience, who would still have been shocked by the innovation of degrading a Greek noblewoman so). Again, Euripides can depict slaves as feeling an almost filial affection for a mistress who has always treated them with human kindness, not as chattels.

The bestowal of Electra on an uninfluential peasant is a reminder that Greek marriages were not affairs of the heart but of arrangement; a Greek girl had to marry the man of papa's choice. The attitude of the Greek male to his womenfolk contained a strong admixture of contempt and fear; it was a man's duty to marry for the sake of offspring to continue the house, but the prospect of taking a wife was not a particularly joyous one. Herodotus tells of a king of Lydia who was actually in love with his own wife, and who thought her the most beautiful woman in the world. But Herodotus found this a matter for surprise, and the majority would probably have assented to Lord Bacon's gloomy summary of the male situation:

> Domesticke cares afflict the husbands bed,
>   or paines his head:
> Those that liue single take it for a curse,
>   or do things worse.
> Some would have children, those that have them, mone,
>   or wish them gone.
> What is it then to haue or haue no wife,
> But single thraldome, or a double strife?

One might of course be very lucky and get a paragon like Penelope; and Hector and Andromache in the *Iliad* provide a tender and delightful picture of conjugal affection. Even so, in the farewell scene from which I have already quoted, Andromache expresses her concern for Hector in quite philotimous terms, as the mainstay of her social status. Contrasted with this in the same poem is the union of Paris with the runaway Helen, entirely an affair of passionate physical attraction. In sexual relationships there was a gap between the married state, instituted by an impersonal society governed by *philotimia*, and the 'love-affair', the urge of *thymos* to be coupled with this or that body. This gap was to be filled by 'romantic' love: love for the other which will survive the other's loss of social and sexual advantages – what has been called love for the other as a *person.*

We sense 'romantic' love in the so-called 'new' comedy of the fourth century BC, where the young master sighs ineffectually after some slave-girl: he wants to *marry* her. Aristophanes and the 'old' comedians of the preceding century would have made him tumble her in the yard, and that would have been that; but this would have offended the new sensibility, which felt a respect for the person of the beloved, yet still compromised with the socially accepted attitude of *philotimia* by finally having the girl revealed as being of impeccable birth, but kidnapped and sold into slavery when a tot – thus removing the last obstacle to wedlock. This is the beginning of the conventional fairy-tale ending, 'and they lived happily ever after'. It reflects the life-story of Eumaeus the swineherd in the *Odyssey*; the interesting novelty is the equation of happiness (or of the highest form of it) with the permanent union of a male and a female.

Perhaps romantic love manifested itself first in European history in the circle of the poetess Sappho, from the island of Lesbos. Her poems to her girlfriends are filled with a refined tenderness which can only be described as personal – for the nature of their relationship was one into which neither *philotimia* nor philoprogenitiveness could enter; it had neither a biological nor a social function, as conventional marriage did. The earliest approximation to such a relationship (in marriage) between the sexes may be that match between Hipparchia and the Cynic philosopher Crates; the couple whose innocent abandon in the act of love, recalling the shamelessness of Eden before the Fall, has been mentioned earlier.

Hipparchia was a woman, well-born (in philotimous terms), who was young in the dying years of the fourth century BC. She became passionately enamoured of Crates's *mental* prowess, and determined to marry him. Her parents objected, but by now parents were becoming more complacent towards their children's wishes in such a matter, so they did all they could to deter her, without forbidding her outright. They even engaged the assistance of Crates himself, who is said to have tried to help them by suddenly revealing himself naked to the maiden, with the admonition that *this* was what she would be taking: the man himself, with no philotimous trappings. She took him.

This extraordinary union was more than a nine-days' wonder: its fame echoed down antiquity. Four hundred years later the philosopher Epictetus referred to it in a passage which illustrates well the conventional view of marriage in the ancient world, and highlights that of Crates and Hipparchia in contrast.

Epictetus had been asked whether one who professed the Cynic philosophy ought to marry as a matter of principle. His reply reads like a plea for a celibate clergy:

> Given a community of wise and sensible men, there would seem to be no reason why anyone should rush to profess the

Cynic way of life. He would benefit no one by so doing. Still, let us imagine the Cynic in such a situation: there would be nothing to stop him marrying and having children, for his wife and his in-laws would be Cynics too, and his children would be brought up as Cynics – why not? But things being what they are the Cynic must see himself as a soldier: with one objective before his eyes, to be the servant of God; free to do his rounds among his fellowmen because he is unshackled by his own concerns and free of ties which, disregarded, would ruin his image as a respectable citizen, but, observed, would make nonsense of his role as messenger, eye and herald of heaven.

Think of all the chores the married man must do in the home, minding the baby and running errands for his wife: how will such a one have time for the cure of souls, to be a psychotherapist and a spiritual ruler? 'Yes, but Crates married, and he was a Cynic.' 'Ah, the case of Crates was an exceptional one, caused by the virus of love, and his wife was another Crates; we are speaking now of typical, uncomplicated marriage in the world as it is, and this we do not find to be enjoined upon the Cynic as a matter of principle.'

A feature of romantic love is the sensitivity of the lover to the moods of the beloved, an ability to put one's self in the other's place and feel with him or her – what has been called *empathy*. A signal development of this faculty in the fifth century was marked by the flowering of drama, especially tragic drama.

It is a commonplace that play is basically the trying-out, under other trappings and in a situation where the consequences of failure will not be too harmful, of a role which may have to be acted upon the stage of life, where to bungle it could prove disastrous. Company is not a necessity for such play; a solitary child is often playwright, cast and audience in a self-sufficient act. But of course it does not have to be a child: the artist is doing it with more subtlety and complexity, hiving himself off into many selves, and feeling them, not merely as agents peripheral to himself, but as the objects of actions directed upon them from outside.

Any narrator, any author, who makes his characters speak for themselves is doing it; the dramatist does nothing but it. The classical Greeks became *conscious* of this faculty, the essence of which children and artists have in the marrow of their bones. Aristotle, in his *Poetics*, emphasised its importance. Not only should a playwright compose with the scene always before his mind's eye, but he should try to 'get inside' his characters and feel the emotions they are supposed to be feeling, if he is to carry conviction. Aristotle shrewdly adds that the poet is akin to the genius or the madman, for the genius is highly adaptable and the madman 'beside himself' – both, in different ways, get outside themselves and the limits of their own natures.

The same theory was being aired before Aristotle was born. In one of his comedies Aristophanes puts it in the mouth of Agathon, a tragedian and a friend of Socrates. Aristophanes presents him as an epicene and precious creature, whose foppish dress and uncertain sex provide the comedian with matter for much ribaldry. Agathon justifies himself by pleading that he is writing a play about women, and is trying to get the feel of it. 'I dress to match my frame of mind. For a poet must trim his ways to harmonise with the work he is engaged on.'

No doubt the theory belonged to the real Agathon, no less than the effeminacy – the joke would not have been very funny otherwise; an appropriate theory, we may think, for one whose sympathies must have been unusually wide.

It was in the fifth century too that a new word made its appearance: *philanthropia*, 'philanthropy', 'love for other men' not because they are your friends rather than your enemies, but because they are men. It was a particular outcrop of the notion of the interrelationship of all things, helped perhaps by the philosophical search for a single underlying substance of all, and implied by the Pythagoreans when they termed the fire which they postulated at the centre of the universe 'the Hearth', as if the world were a house sheltering a family.

Philanthropia was the nearest Greek word for what the Romans were to call *humanitas*, that humane fellow-feeling which distinguishes human beings from brutes. But whereas the Romans saw this as the hall-mark of *homo sapiens*, for the Greeks this hall-mark was something else: his *sapientia*, or reasoning power, in fact.

With the birth of philosophy, and from it logic, men came to see themselves as distinguished from animals by possessing not merely a sense of *diké*, 'justice', as Hesiod had put it, but also by possessing reason: the ability to choose their goals and the means to reach them, and to discern and describe such purposeful activity outside themselves, in the behaviour of other men or in the workings of the physical world. The workings of the latter seemed to be explicable in terms of purpose or function, therefore the world must be the handiwork of a rational creator, and Man's possession of reason, which separated him from the beasts, related him to God, the creator or orderer. Reason, it was thought, is the divine element in us, and its purest exercise the most godlike activity of which we are capable.

There was a tale that Pythagoras once visited a certain ruler called Leon who, amazed by the man's learning, asked him in what special skill he had been educated. Pythagoras answered that he knew no skill, but was a philosopher. Struck by the novelty of the name, Leon inquired how philosophers differed from the rest of men. 'Life,' Pythagoras replied, 'is like the games whither men flock from all over Greece, some to win prizes by athletic prowess, others attracted by the profit to be made by trading there; while there are yet others, and these the most independent, who seek neither applause nor gain, but who come to watch and see what goes on, and how. Just so are we come into this life from another life of a different kind, like visitors from a foreign city to some fair, some of us enslaved to love of fame, others to love of money, and a very few, who despise these things, come to contemplate nature; these call themselves Wisdom's men, that is, philosophers. And as at the games they are freest who are mere spectators seeking nothing for themselves, so in life the disinterested study and understanding of nature far excels all other pursuits.' For this is to study the work of the only true craftsman, God.

Though it is quite likely that Pythagoras did coin the word 'philosopher', the authority for the above story was a pupil of Plato, and it may have been invented in Plato's circle. Noteworthy in the story is the likening of the philosopher to an onlooker at the games: another pupil of Plato, Aristotle, must have had this in mind when he wrote his great panegyric of the contemplative life, the life of the 'onlooker', which is the exercise of Man's proper ability, reason, in its purest form; purest, because it is done for its own sake and not for the sake of some object beyond itself (as opposed, for example, to 'business', which men undertake not for its own sake in Aristotle's view, but for an object beyond it – for example to make money).

'If happiness,' says Aristotle, 'accompanies the exercise of *areté*, the realisation of potential, it would reasonably be the most superior *areté* it accompanies, and this would be the *areté* of the best thing in us. Whether this is reason or something else, which we think to be our natural leader and guide and to be able to conceive of the beautiful and the divine (because it either is itself divine or is the most godlike element in us), the exercise of its special *areté* would produce perfect happiness. As I have said, its special *areté* is contemplative, or speculative . . . The exercise of speculation is the highest exercise (reason is the supreme faculty of our minds, and the objects of reason are the supreme mental objects); it is also the most persistent faculty, for we can persist in speculation longer than in any action (so in this respect also it is the most godlike activity open to us, for God is not tired by his activity).

'We also think that happiness must have an admixture of pleasure, and of all the exercises of *areté* the exercise of the scientific faculty is allowed to give the most pleasure; at least we think the pleasures of philosophy to be quite remarkably refined and lasting . . . It is here too that we come nearest to what has been called "self-sufficiency" : true, the philosopher, the just man and the rest all must have the necessities of life, but given these the just man will also need a subject and instruments for the exercise of his justice, similarly with the temperate man and the brave man; whereas the philosopher can speculate on his own – indeed, he will be the more aided by solitude the better philosopher he is. No doubt, with assistants he would achieve even more, but still he comes nearest of all to self-sufficiency. And speculation would seem to be the only activity to give satisfaction for itself alone; for nothing accrues from it beyond itself, whereas from the practical *aretai* (virtues) we acquire something in some degree over and above the exercise of them.

'Moreover, happiness would seem to lie in relaxation: for we work to have leisure, as we war to have peace; so the exercise of the practical *aretai* is in the directing of a state or an army, either of which is "business" – in the latter case unrelieved (for no one chooses or prepares war for its own sake: only a ruffian would make friends into enemies just to have a fight); but the governor of a state too is "busy", inasmuch as, over and above the activity of governing, he aims at the acquisition of power and prestige (*philotimia*) or the happiness of himself and his fellow-citizens, which clearly is sought as an object of the activity over and above the activity itself.

'If then of all exercises of *areté* those exercises in the governance of citizens or troops are fairest and greatest, but these are not desirable for their own sake but for some further aim and involve "business", while the exercise of reason, being speculative, we accept as being more inherently valuable, aiming at no end beyond itself, bringing its own peculiar pleasure (which actually boosts the activity), and making the man as self-sufficient, relaxed and tranquil as a man can be, with all other attributes of the blessed: then this would constitute man's most happy state – given a complete span of years (for happiness implies nothing incomplete). Such a life would be more than human, depending as it would not on the human but on the divine in man, the exercise of which excels the exercise of any other *areté* as it itself, being simple, excels the compound.

'If then reason is the divine aspect of man, the life of reasoning is the divine life for man. We must take no notice of those who tell us to trim our thoughts to our humanity and mortality; but we must be gods as far as it lies in our power to be, and strive to live by the supreme faculty in us; for even if its bulk be tiny, yet its power and value are the greatest – a point which every man would concede, if it is true that that which governs is also better. So it would be strange indeed if a man were to choose not his proper life but another's . . . For that which is proper to each by nature is best and pleasantest to him. That which is proper to man is the life of reasoning, if it is true that man is pre-eminently reasonable. This therefore is the happiest life.'

Aristotle's argument is the crown of that thinking which linked Man with God through their common possession of reason. Though theoretically Aristotle's claim for philosophising as the supreme human activity may seem to be made for all men, in practice no doubt he would consider it to be confined to certain men who were 'free by nature'. The Pythagoreans had a saying that 'the kinds of rational being are three – gods, men and creatures like Pythagoras' – these last being clearly philosophers, who are thus given a status between gods and ordinary men, which is the status of 'demons'. Some such distinction is indeed implied in the fabled discourse of Pythagoras to Leon.

Aristotle's magnificent apologia was a telling shot in the battle beween philosophy and rhetoric, which had broken out between Plato and his followers and the followers of Gorgias, the 'father of rhetoric' whom we have already met debating the merits of his subject with Socrates. This quarrel was to be a chronic one, and indeed its after-taste is still with us, not only in the awe accorded to philosophers but in the pejorative flavour of the word *rhetoric*, as if the sole function of rhetoric were to paint falsehood in false colours so as to look like truth, and 'rhetorical' were the mere equivalent of 'meretricious'. Yet in the art of communication rhetoric takes precedence over philosophy (if philosophy is to be defined as purely rational), inasmuch as it can do what reason cannot: it can commend to another person a sketch of the foundation on which reason can build, it can carry a conviction of reason's premises. One can look at the same picture upside-down or downside-up, and experience a very different effect from it; one can look at the same world standing on one's feet or on one's head, with similar consequences: rhetoric can convince you that one stance is better than another, or suggest to you a new stance, which reason unaided cannot. Somehow, rhetoric appeals to nature, that fluid concept – or perhaps it is rather individual natures it appeals to; in which case our individual reactions to it should be worthy of remark. There are those, for instance, who will be delighted to be told that

man is a risen ape; others may find satisfaction in the contemplation of him as a fallen angel; while recent years have seen the
emergence of another class, whose peculiar joy it is to see him
as a fallen ape. And each age or culture has its arch-rhetoric,
appearing to it not as such but as an angel of light, or ultimate
court of appeal; its lie in the heart, its essence and ultimately
its poison. In one age it may be patriotism, in another authority;
in the Technological Age it is statistics.

Though Aristotle was the apostle *par excellence* of Speculative
Reason, and indeed chiefly responsible for present-day Western
man's unjustifiable pride in his own rationality (which he has
managed to combine with a contempt for Aristotle), it was the
pantheistic Stoics who, following leads gleaned from Heraclitus,
the Pythagoreans and Plato, saw the natural universe as the
perfect object of Reason's exercise, in which Man, the microcosm,
the Little Cosmos, can learn about himself by studying the
macrocosm, the Great Cosmos, which he reflects. A fine expression of this idea is in an astrological poem by a Roman Stoic
of the beginning of our era, some three centuries after
Aristotle:

Now Nature is nowhere hidden, but is transparent to us.
We have captured and mastered the universe; we children of
Nature now understand our parent, the part understands the
whole, and we reach back to the stars whence we came. For
there can be no doubt that God dwells within our breasts, no
doubt that our souls came from heaven and return there, and
that, just as the physical world is a receptacle for divine mind
which suffuses and steers the whole, so our physical bodies
too are the hospices of mind, which rules supreme and orders
the whole man. What wonder that men can come to understand the workings of the world, seeing that they are little
worlds in themselves, and each one of us is an image of God
in miniature! It is wrong to think that Man's stock is anything but divine. All other creatures, of land or sea or air,
look downwards; their good is sensual, they have no reason
and no speech: Man, the lord of all, is the only one of her
offspring Nature has reared to be able to investigate her, to
have speech and a genius to match the task. He has congregated

in cities, yoked the earth to bear crops, tamed the animals, laid a road over the sea; he alone holds erect his head, the citadel of Reason, and in the pride of victory directs to the stars his starlike eyes, inspects heaven from a nearer vantage-point, and scans God himself . . . and in probing the body of his kin seeks out himself in the stars . . . The heavens themselves invite our inspection, display the laws that govern them and do not suffer themselves to be hid. How can it be wrong to unravel an open secret? And do not despise your ability to do so, because it is confined in a tiny body . . . Do not assess Reason by the body that cabins it, or by Reason's weight, but by its strength: *Reason can conquer everything.*

Ratio omnia vincit. It is the beginning of the Faustian urge in man to understand and master his environment, to control his destiny, the beginning of his arrogant pride in the efficacy of his own rationality, driving him on like an undying flame. It is what drove Dante's Ulysses on, as the spirit of Ulysses related to Dante in hell, a spirit in no human form but a flickering tongue of ever-burning, never-consuming flame. It drove Ulysses on, this desire for understanding, this pursuit of the virtue, excellence, the *areté*, of Man, so different from the animals: *fatti non foste a viver come bruti, ma per seguir virtute e canoscenza,* overcoming the weakness of old age, fear of hardship, familial love, it drove him into the unknown southern hemisphere, until he saw a strange mountain rising to heaven from the sea. It was the mountain of Purgatory, but it was not to be attained by the lonely pride of Reason. A storm bursts from it, 'whirled the ship round three times, and the fourth time lifted the poop aloft and plunged the prow below, and the sea closed over it'.

Noticeable now are the stirrings of a sort of active spiritual discontent. Pessimism over what is called today 'the human situation' was as old as Homer, but it was a pessimism tempered by resignation to what was accepted as the general doom of mankind. Now the individual is beginning to resent his own peculiar lot, and becoming restless: how he wishes he were someone else! So Phaedra, in the *Hippolytus* of Euripides, sickened by a hopeless love, longs romantically for the solace of hunting and the joys of the countryside; longs to share the pursuits of her unattainable beloved, which are the pursuits of men – and of the goddess Artemis, the virgin huntress and arch-enemy of the passion which enthrals Phaedra.

The most remarkable expressions of this frustration and the *ennui* which sometimes accompanies it are to be found in Roman writers. Horace, who died in 8 BC, notes how men tend to envy each other's occupations: the man of business wishes he were a simple farmer, the soldier longs for the safety and the rewards of a merchant's life – how easily the other fellow has it compared with me! Just so, 'when we are in town we want to be in the country, but when we are there we switch our allegiance and praise town to the skies'. The case is graphically put by the Epicurean poet Lucretius, a generation before Horace:

If only men, as they feel the weight on their mind which wears them out with its heaviness, could as easily realise from what cause it comes and why such a lump of ill clutters their breast, they would not live as we see they often do, not knowing what they want and always longing to be somewhere else, as if they could rid themselves of their burden thus. Often one who is sick of staying in his spacious home sallies out, and as quickly returns, for outside he feels no better. He drives out to his country villa, as fast as if he was a fire-engine; but as soon as he has crossed the threshold he yawns, or nods off to sleep to forget it all, or even makes for town again hell-for-leather. In doing this he is trying to escape from himself, but of course he cannot, so with ill grace he clings to the self and hates it, because sick as he is he does not know the cause of his sickness.

(As Horace said, 'those who go running off abroad get a change of climate but not a change of heart'.)

This is an excellent description of accidie, the loss of interest in life; Dante's *accidioso fummo*, 'smoky apathy', whose sluggard victims gurgle beneath the mire in the Fifth Circle of hell because their hearts were choked with grumbling resentment when they were in 'the sweet air and the glad light of the sun'.

Accidie was castigated in the Middle Ages as the sin of sloth, whose onslaught was so deadly that it was ascribed to that 'noonday devil' of the psalmist, as dangerous an adversary as 'the Thing that walks in the darkness'. There is a most interesting account of the symptoms in John Cassian's *Rules of Monastic Life*, written soon after AD 400.

The first sign is that the monk takes a violent dislike to his surroundings; he finds his cell disgusting and his colleagues contemptible. He becomes listless, and cannot work on his own, or sit reading in his room. He is miserable because he feels that he is making no spiritual progress, benefiting no one else by his instruction when he could have done so. He wishes he were in another monastery a long way off, where they manage things much better; here the chances of salvation are nil. Then, about noon, he is overcome by intense fatigue and hunger, as if he had just returned from a long journey or hard labour, or had not eaten for several days. Now he waits anxiously for one of his colleagues to call on him, and keeps going out of his cell to see what time it is; nothing, it seems, will cure him but a visit from a neighbour, or a nap. Finally he feels that anything is better than sitting here uselessly; he must drop in on a fellow-monk for a chat, or do his duty by visiting the sick or the elderly further afield, or by ministering to the needs of some sister in the spirit who has no parents to lean on.

But accidie is a neurotic extreme, a feeling of the purposelessness of one's life – of life in general. In its beginnings, or sub-acute stages, it impelled men to try to master their environment and re-mould it closer to the dimly-felt desire of their hearts. A remarkable essay in this direction was the adornment of private houses with mosaic floors – the equivalent of patterned carpets – with frescoes or wall-paintings, with statues – hitherto the appurtenances of temples or of public places – and with pleasure-gardens.

'Gardens were before Gardeners, and but some hours after the earth'; but Sir Thomas Browne was referring to the Garden of Eden, where the Lord God took his ease: Greek gardens were longer evolving. The first one to be described is that of King Alcinous, Odysseus's host when he was among the easy-living Phaeacians:

Tall vigorous trees grew there – pear and pomegranate and fair-fruiting apple, the sweet fig and luxuriant olive. Their crop never failed throughout the year, winter or summer, but always some were budding under Zephyr's breath, as others ripened; pear matured on pear, apple on apple, one grape-cluster succeeded another, fig succeeded fig. There too was planted his fertile vineyard: here, on a level spot, grapes were drying in the sun's heat, there the harvesters were at work, here the treaders; fronting them were grapes still unripe, while others were just tinged with red.

By the orchard's verge were orderly beds of all kinds of green stuff, stocked continuously; and there were two springs, one irrigating the garden, the other gushing towards the lofty palace, by its courtyard gate, whence the townsmen drew their water.

So splendidly had the gods endowed Alcinous's house.

Before the days of canning and refrigeration it needed a divine dispensation to supply Alcinous's vegetable-cook throughout the year; just so, I suppose, the Olympians never wanted for greengroceries. But the utilitarian nature of Alcinous's demesne will be noted; there are no flowers. It is in the gardens of the gods, around their temples, that such refined amenities are first to be found, as witness Sappho's words in a hymn to the goddess of love:

Aphrodite, I pray you, leave Crete for our holy temple here, where an orchard of your favourite apples invites you, and the perfume of frankincense is on the altars, and cool streams babble among the fruit-twigs, and nowhere is without the shade of rose-bushes, and one drifts into sleep charmed by the rustling leaves.

The earliest Greek gardens belonged to gods or to (godlike) kings. Even so, the king's garden was directed to the practical end of food-producing; unnecessary luxuries, such as the scent of roses, were entirely the privilege of the immortal gods. But move on half a millennium, and we hear Virgil telling of the pleasure which even a retired pirate had from the flowers he cultivated among his vegetables:

Close by the turreted walls of Taranto, where Galaesus with its black waters suckles the yellowing cornfields, I remember coming upon an old Cilician, the owner of a patch of ground which nobody else wanted, for it was neither fit for pasture nor well-disposed to the vine. Yet that old man, cropping the occasional vegetable among the brambles, the white lily here and there, odd greenery and the humble poppy, was as rich as a king in the mind's delights, and when he returned to his cottage late in the evening would load his table with good things which had cost him nothing. In spring he was the first with his roses, in autumn with his apples; and, when scowling winter was still splitting rocks with its frost and checking watercourses with its icy bridle, he would already be cutting the tender larkspur, grumbling at the late summer and Zephyr's coyness.

Outside the gardens of Greek temples, a few kinds of flowers were cultivated (at any rate from the fifth century onwards), but commercially, to meet the demand for garlands at dinner-parties, rather than for admiration *in situ*. The amenities most valued in a Mediterranean summer were water and shade, and the city (or its benefactors) provided trees and fountains for the Athenian public of the fifth century. It was not until the next century that private individuals began to lay out gardens on their own account. The Athenian soldier-adventurer Xenophon made an elaborate one while in exile, perhaps inspired by the 'paradises' of the Persian king, some of which he had seen. Part of it was cultivable land, part stocked with wild animals for hunting. Its centre was a temple of the huntress Artemis, and those of the general public who enjoyed it were expected to pay a tithe to her. Flowers are not mentioned.

'God-centred' too were 'the groves of Academe', where Plato taught, and the walks of Apollo's Lyceum which shaded Aristotle and his Peripatetics. The first (or, if not the first, the most famous) *secular* garden, set in urban surroundings, was that made by Epicurus – that connoisseur of the art of living, who banished the gods from human affairs. The planting of miniature gardens in pots, starting as an observance in the festival of the god Adonis (introduced to Athens from the east at the end of the fifth century), became a popular pastime; and later, in Rome, even the poor had their window-boxes.

The same age which saw men beginning to use such dominion as they had over their environment to make it more heaven-like also saw their ambition take a bolder and more curious turn. Not content to be the gods' equals, some sought, through the art of magic, to command them.

At first it had been a god's prerogative alone to control nature or to be free of nature's bonds: to shake the earth, to summon the storm, to fly through the air, to change the shape of himself or another, and so on. Then these powers were allowed to certain 'divine' men – ascribed, for instance, to Pythagoras, implied for himself by Empedocles. The miracles recounted of Pythagoras included not only marvellous prophecies but a strange authority over wild animals and the ability to vanish, and to appear in two widely-separated places at once. We still have the verses with which Empedocles concluded his poem *On Nature*, in which he promises his pupil supernatural powers:

> You shall learn all the drugs which are a defence against illness and old age . . . You shall lull the tireless might of the winds, whose onslaught destroys the cornfields, and in turn, if you wish, you shall bring back their blasts. Out of the dark tempest you shall make a timely drought for men, and out of drought summer rains that pour down from the skies and feed the trees. You shall bring back from the House of Death a man in all his strength.

We have another example of the wonderful power which contact with the divine, or possession by a god, can confer upon mortals in the shepherd's account to his king of the Maenads' behaviour in Euripides's *Bacchantes*: not only did wild creatures show them a marvellous docility – the women used live snakes for belts, and suckled fawns and wolf cubs – but inanimate nature responded to them in no ordinary way:

> One struck a rock with her staff, and from it spouted a dewy stream of water. Another stabbed the earth with hers, and the god sent up for her a jet of wine. Such as longed for a draught of milk scraped the ground with their fingers

and milk gushed forth; while their ivy-clad wands dripped
with honey.

With a touch of homeliness the shepherd prefaces his announce-
ment with the words 'I have come to tell you about the wild
women, sire, how they are doing strange things that would beat
a conjuring show'. Such shows would be familiar to Euripides's
audience. They were men's first modest attempts to usurp, or to
seem to usurp, the gods' exemption from the restrictive trammels
of nature's laws. They comprised a variety of entertainments of
the sort one sees at fairs, which could be witnessed for a small
payment: singers, performing animals, acrobats, jugglers and
conjurers. It was the feats of the last-named which seemed
miraculous; they included fire-eating, sword-swallowing, thimble-
rigging, and causing cows and horses to exchange heads.

The later Greeks did sometimes set up statues to specially
gifted professors of such prestidigitation, but it is not likely that
they considered them really to have divine powers. Indeed Celsus,
writing against Christianity in the second century, uses their
example to depreciate the weight which his opponent gave to
the miracles of Jesus (against Jesus's own advice): 'Let us
grant' Celsus says, 'that the healings and the raising of the dead
and the feeding of the multitude really happened: these are like
the works of the magicians and the pupils of the Egyptians, who
in the market-place sell for a few pence their solemn mumbo-
jumbo, and drive out demons from men, and puff away diseases,
and call up the souls of heroes, and display to us lavish feasts
that are not really there, and objects that simulate the motions
of life but are not really alive: surely you will not ask us to
believe that the people who do this sort of thing are the sons of
God?'

Such were the tricks of the conjurers; yet such, according
to Aristotle, were quite foreign to the original *magicians*, the
Persian Magi.

Of the beliefs and practices of the first Magi we know almost
nothing. They seem to have concerned themselves with narrow-
minded ritual, and purifications, especially in connection with
dead bodies. The importation of their religious ideas from Persia
into Europe the ancients associated with the invasion of Xerxes,

whose companion, the magus Ostanes, 'substituted the moral standards of monsters for those of men'. Herodotus, the historian of the Persian invasions, gives us no inkling of this sinister reputation: for him the magi are priestly interpreters of omens. But in the tragedians who were Herodotus's contemporaries *magus* is a term of abuse.

By the turn of the fifth century the magi have joined forces with the miracle-men and the conjurers, in the eyes of our Greek sources. The author of the medical treatise *On the Sacred Disease* writes: 'My own view is that those who first attributed a sacred character to epilepsy were like the magicians, purifiers, charlatans and quacks of our own day, men who claim great piety and superior knowledge', who 'profess to know how to bring down the moon, to eclipse the sun, to make storm and sunshine, rain and drought, the sea impassable and the earth barren, and so on', by magic and sacrifice.

There was a legend that Xerxes, in the course of his invasion of Greece, was entertained by the father of Democritus, chief pioneer of the atomic theory, and in return left behind some magi to be tutors to the boy. According to another legend, when in Egypt Democritus was initiated into the magicians' mysteries by Ostanes. He is also said to have been taught by a Pythagorean and to have written a laudatory work on the wondrous Pythagoras himself.

There is still in existence a very brief booklet called *The Tricks of Democritus*. It is the merest trifle, but the first item is 'How to make bronze look like gold' – and we are witnessing the humble origins of chemistry.

Democritus, Pythagoras, Ostanes and the magi were all in the Hellenistic era and in the Alexandria of the Ptolemies – that is, in the centuries immediately before the Christian era – to become associated with the beginnings of alchemy. The trend is epitomised in the person of one Anaxilaus, called by Jerome 'a Pythagorean and magician', and banished from Italy by the emperor Augustus about 27 BC – no doubt from fear of his occult powers. These do not in fact appear to have been very great: he seems to have been an adept at giving a sort of after-dinner cabaret performance. He would carry round a basin of glowing cinders and sulphur, which made the guests look like corpses; and he had other nostrums, to make them appear to have the countenances of negroes or the heads of asses. A place is confirmed for him among the first alchemists by a magical papyrus, which says that he ascribed the (alchemical) creation of silver to Democritus.

From this same Augustan period a curious document has been preserved which shows that wonderworking on a grand scale was moving from the marketplace to the temple; the holy miraclemonger was aided by the conjurer and the scientist. This is a letter, professedly from one Thessalus to Caesar, in which the writer describes how he sought, and was granted, a personal interview with a god. Thessalus had studied at Alexandria, where he became deeply interested in medicine, and particularly in a work of the Pharaoh Nechepso on the healing properties of plants and stones. He tried recipe after recipe but continually failed till mortification drove him nearly distracted, and he left Alexandria in shame for Thebes. There he became friendly with the priests, of whom, feeling that the only solution to his problem must come from some divine revelation, he made tentative inquiries about their skill in conjuration. These inquiries met with a cool response, except from one priest. This man, in pity at Thessalus's tearful importunity, agreed to call up the god Asclepius to answer his questions. After a preparatory fast of three days, Thessalus entered a chamber which the priest had prepared, and was commanded to sit down facing a throne. The magician pronounced a mysterious invocation, and the god appeared seated upon the throne, in unspeakable beauty and splendour of apparel. He graciously saluted his client (who was almost paralysed by awe), asked his wishes, and answered his questions.

We need not suppose Thessalus to be lying, but to be advertising a fraud. In an Alexandrian work on optics of the first century AD (the introduction of which has a Pythagoran tone) there is a section headed 'How to place a mirror in a given position so that any who approaches will see in it neither himself nor anyone else, but only a pre-selected image'. Instructions are then given for the production of an appearance, or *epiphany*, of a god in a temple: a person dressed as the god stands behind the altar, at a lower level; when he is illuminated his reflection is cast by a concealed mirror, set obliquely, upon another above the altar. In a slightly refined form the principle was used as recently as last century in the illusion known as 'Pepper's Ghost'.

It was the second and succeeding centuries of our era that saw the zenith of religious frauds. Among the effects we hear of the reading of sealed messages (with the seal apparently unbroken), or of messages written in an invisible medium such as water; self-sacrificing sheep, which cut their own throats before the altar; making a skull speak; and the production of fiery apparitions.

This last featured in the seances of the self-styled 'theurgists' – a name which could mean 'those who make gods' or 'those who work by means of gods'. The aim of the original theurgists of the second century AD was to evoke gods, who either spoke through a medium or manifested in fiery shapes. 'Pronounce this formula,' says the Neo-Platonist Proclus, quoting a theurgic poem, 'and you will see "an appearance of fire like a boy, stretched over the billows of air, dancing; or fire unshaped, whence a voice proceeds; or a wealth of light whirling with a whistle about the area; or you may see a horse flashing with a supernatural brightness, or a boy riding on the back of a horse, afire, or decked with gold, or naked, or perhaps shooting from a bow and standing on the horse's back." '

The theurgists may not have been trying to conjure up the gods in order to control them (like the magicians), but for the sake of their company; an attempt to recall, for unluckier and more sophisticated men, those happy far-off days of the Golden Age, when gods moved easily among men as a matter of course, and shared their tables and their counsel.

Fourth-century philosophers mooted plans to realise that harmonious society of legend, to establish Utopia among us now. Formerly it had been inaccessible, beyond a gulf of time or space: it existed 'once upon a time', or in a Never-never Land of some unchartable fringe of the world. Now, men began to hope that they could create it in their midst.

It would be fruitless to ask whether Hesiod or Empedocles really believed that their Golden Age had once been historical fact, or whether Homer really thought that he himself, if he put himself out a bit, could pay a visit to Elysium or his idealised Phaeacians. But no doubt a visit to the Abii was possible – that northern tribe whose exceptional fairmindedness (or 'justice') Homer remarks in the same sentence in which he mentions the savage (and very real) Thracians.

Even further north than the Abii, so far north in fact that they lived 'beyond the North Wind (Boreas)', were said to be the Hyperboreans, so just and so idyllic that the poets would have it that the artistic god Apollo took his holidays among them. And in the seventh century, not long after Homer, when explorers were probing the northern coast of the Black Sea, one Greek at least was so convinced of the actual existence of the Hyperboreans that he plunged into the unknown regions of the steppes to try to find them. Not surprisingly, he failed; but he did get as far as western Siberia, where he heard rumours of his goal (rumours of Chinese civilisation, perhaps), and also of such daunting terrors besetting the path ahead that he turned back.

This attempt, though it did not succeed, at least testified that some men had come to think of Paradise as here and now; or rather, now but elsewhere. But if it *could* exist elsewhere, why should it not exist here? From the end of the fifth century BC, in the confidence which men had newly found in themselves, philosophers were producing blueprints for the ideal society. The first hint we have of them is in comic parodies, but a serious sample still exists in Plato's *Republic* (otherwise entitled *On Justice* [or *Right Action*]).

Plato, influenced by Pythagorean ideas, saw an analogy between physical, mental and social health; for him 'the health of the body politic' was more than a metaphor. Just as our bodies are organisms whose well-being depends on a harmonious functioning, or working together, of their parts, and the well-being of our souls (*psychai*) consists in the harmonious functioning of the soul's rational, sensual and passionate elements, so the state's well-being lies in the co-operation or concord of the classes which it comprises. Plato thought that his Utopia could be conjured into existence by law – by a legally constituted polity; it would not be an aristocracy in the old accepted sense, but rather what modern parlance terms a 'meritocracy', where there would be mobility between the classes, but a mobility controlled by capabilities, and the classes would possess political power in proportion to their possession of intellect (the 'philosopher kings'), and material wealth in inverse proportion to their possession of power.

Story has it that Plato was offered the opportunity by the admiring tyrant of Syracuse to try out his ideas on the tyrant's city: 'Treat my kingdom as if it were your own.' The experiment was an ignominious failure, and the crestfallen philosopher ended as a bargain in the Syracusan slave-market, whence he was lucky to be redeemed by his friends in Athens.

Plato's ideal republic was conceived, naturally enough, very much on the lines of the tight-knit Greek *polis*, or city-state, which he knew. There is nothing cosmopolitan about it. In contrast to the ideal state of Plato, we have only second-hand knowledge of that of Zeno the Stoic, propounded soon after Plato's death. But from the scanty reference to it we can deduce that its citizens were to be 'the wise'; that it was to be cosmopolitan, not in the sense of being a 'world-state', but in the sense of being of world-wide occurrence (that is, it could occur among barbarians as well as Greeks); that such ideal states would lack the rivalry of philotimous trappings consisting in powerful armaments and splendid public buildings; that philotimous jealousies between families within the states would also cease, for there would be no vying in wealth because there would be no money – and there would be no families either, for the limitation of relationships which the family imposes would disappear through sexual promiscuity, in a society where men and women would not be distinguished even by differences of dress; and, finally, that the god who inspired and moved the whole community would be Eros – Love.

Perhaps the most interesting of Zeno's conceptions is this last – that his ideal citizens should be moved by love for each other. The bond between them was to come from something within each individual, not dependent upon the behest of the law or even on an astute appeal to common interests. Doubtless it had to some extent been anticipated by Empedocles's Golden Age, when Aphrodite the goddess of love reigned supreme and man lived on terms of genial fellowship with all other creatures; but more than a century separated Zeno from Empedocles, and we must not forget the early, and persistent, fusion of the idea of 'friendship' with the sharing of interests: you are my friend (for the moment, anyway), because our interests happen to coincide. This is to be distinguished from saying that our interests coincide because we are friends, or love each other.

In a number of ways, then, the New Man was a being between two planes, in a state of tension. He felt himself as more than human, but less than divine. His divinity was marred by one thing in particular, his mortality; and heightened self-awareness brought with it as a corollary a heightened concern with its opposite, self-extinction. A by-product of this was a new phenomenon: hypochondria, a neurotic solicitude about self-preservation, reflected in a preoccupation with illness and death.

For our finest example of an ancient hypochondriac we must move down the centuries, to a Greek who lived under the Roman empire in the second century AD: that Aelius Aristeides, whose delirium was once comforted by the appearance at his bedside of the goddess Athena in panoply.

On that occasion he was in the throes of smallpox; but over a period of thirty years or more he suffered from symptoms which are not to be diagnosed so readily – which medical science today would class as 'psychosomatic'. He was so interested in his condition that he kept a diary about it, and even had frequent dreams about it; dreams in which remedies were prescribed to him mysteriously, perhaps by the god Asclepius himself, whose advice he preferred when it conflicted with that of the mere mortal doctors who also attended him. And so effective was the god's therapy (in the end) that in gratitude Aristeides left to posterity, in a book entitled *Sacred Tales*, a full history of his valetudinarian vicissitudes. Here is his account of one episode, which took place long before the smallpox:

At the height of winter and my illness I was at breakfast, when a piercing headache came on, and the muscles of my face were drawn taut, and my lips were locked together, and I felt quite helpless. Doubled up as I was, I rushed into my bedroom and threw myself on the bed anyhow, and a high fever supervened. I could find no relief. My mother and my nurse and the other servants set up a wail; somehow I nodded to most of them to leave, and braced myself against what was to come.

After this it was sunset or a bit later, when on top of the fever I was seized by a fit neither describable nor imaginable: my body was contorted in all manner of ways – my knees were carried up and beat against my head, and my hands jerked uncontrollably and hammered against my throat and face; my chest was thrust forward and my spine plucked backward, like a sail billowing in the wind. No part of my body was at rest, but was mightily changed from its natural condition; my tossings and turnings were the limit, and torments unspeakable were mine, which could not be borne in silence, yet redoubled when I cried out.

All this lasted till midnight and beyond without the least intermission; then I had a respite from the worst, but it was by no means all over. They swathed me in hot blankets and tried every way to make me sweat it out, so that I just scraped through; and before it was dawn someone ran for the doctor. He came a day or so later. And at noon or thereabouts I was subjected to another onslaught, and shortly afterward had a black motion. And when I was on the stool I came over all weak and faint, and perspired horribly. The doctor had got in a fluster and prescribed food, but of course that was not the trouble. When darkness fell it was like being tossed at sea on a stormy night, but I managed to sleep enough to have a dream, in which an order was given me to go to my parents' home and pay my respects to the statue of Zeus nearby; and I seemed to hear voices, and details of how I was to address the god. There was snow everywhere and it was no easy matter to get out, and I had upwards of a quarter of a mile to go; but I mounted a horse and went, and paid my respects, and I was no sooner back than my symptoms disappeared.

On another occasion Asclepius told him through a dream that he would be free of his fit if he ran a mile and dived into water. Aristeides, punctilious in his observance of the god's prescriptions, had the distance to the nearest river measured. It was a mile and a half, so he took a coach for half a mile, ran the rest in the teeth of a north wind, and returned after his immersion muddy but cured.

Twice he looked to die of his ailment, but each time at the crisis point a young relation was carried off by illness, and Aristeides recovered. As he saw it, a life had been taken for his life, and he rejoiced at these signal manifestations of the god's mercy and favour.

A more famous valetudinarian than Aristeides was the Roman Seneca, who lived a century before. He was a man good at heart, racked by his wealth and position, which he felt he should renounce; for he was one of the richest men in the empire, a moneylender with clients as far off as Britain, and was tutor to the emperor Nero himself, whose waywardness his well-meant efforts could not control. Seneca was a paradigm of the philo-timous man who hates *philotimia*:

My ill-health granted me a long respite [he writes in one of his *Letters to Lucilius*] but it has suddenly returned in force. 'What's wrong now?' you will ask. An excellent ques-tion, as there is nothing in the book I haven't had at some time. But one disease especially seems to have made me its own: asthma. Its onset is sharp and sudden; in an hour it is over – luckily: any longer, and it would be all over!

I have had every kind of illness, from the slight upset to the near-fatal; but this beats all. However bad the rest were, they merely put one on a bed of pain; *this* is like being on one's deathbed! No wonder the doctors call it 'practising dying' – for one day my lungs will really do what they have been so long rehearsing.

Do not imagine that your correspondent is overjoyed, and mistakes this escape for a restoration of health. That would be as silly as the defendant who thinks that he has been acquitted because his trial has been adjourned. Yet even when the thing had me in its full stranglehold I found peace in positive thinking. 'Death,' I said to myself, 'by these repeated probes is trying to find out the truth about me; but I long ago found out the truth about death.' When did I do that? Before I was born. Death is non-existence; and I already know what it is like, not to exist. What comes after me will be no different from what came before me, and if there is any unpleasantness to come we must also have experienced it before we came into the world; yet nothing worried us then.

This sounds like one whistling in the dark. How nice if that brazen sleep should be dreamless, if *post mortem* our state should be no different from the ante-natal! Seneca himself put the dilemma more squarely elsewhere: 'See those two over there? One fears that death may be the end, the other fears that it may not be.'

If we move back yet another hundred years, into the first century before Christ, we find the Latin poet Lucretius diagnosing the root cause of man's self-discontent as fear of death. By this Lucretius meant, as his master Epicurus had meant, fear that we may *survive* death; but the significant thing is the new preoccupation with the question of the personal survival of death, and the fact that this preoccupation crystallised during the fourth century BC (Epicurus lived from 341 till 270). Whether this diagnosis was correct matters less, perhaps; that 'divine discontent' which the Epicureans were concerned to cure might have been caused otherwise, by a growing consciousness that man is heir to an inheritance of which he feels himself to be unworthy.

6

Ways of Salvation

'*Mouse* is a word; mice eat cheese; therefore words eat
cheese.' So, if I can't see through this one, what? Shall I
mind to set my mousetraps where they won't catch words? Or
shall I hide my lunch where my book can't eat it? What
childish nonsense: is this what is behind your philosopher's
image, that frown, that beard? Is it for this that the dons'
faces are so pale and long? Yet what does philosophy promise
mankind? It promises good advice. Look at this man: Death
has just called out his name; look at this one, he is festering
in the chains of poverty; and at this other, racked by concern
for money – his own or someone else's. One man fears the
stroke of luck which will take away his fortune, another
longs for it. Here you see a victim of human malice, there of
divine. This is no time for trifling; these people need help.
Why do the philosophers not live up to their grand promises?
With all their fine sayings, how they will teach us not to be
mesmerised either by the gleam of gold or by the flash of
steel, but to rise above common desires and common fears
equally, they act as if they were in the infants' class. Is this
the way to the stars, *sic itur ad astra*? For that is what
philosophy professes, to make us God's equals. Well, we're
waiting: do it.

The charge that Seneca here makes against philosophy, of
mere quibbling, had become something of a commonplace since
the days when a sophist in Plato's *Euthydemus* had proved by
inexorable logic to young Ctesippus that he was his own puppies'
brother. But the science was then young, a rich, exciting, newly-
discovered country, where the glitter of the false syllogism could
not readily be distinguished from gold. We should not suppose
from Plato's parodies that all sophistry was disingenuous. But

by the first century AD the case was somewhat different, and Seneca may be protesting, in a Roman way, against the aridities of Stoic or Sceptic argumentation. Whether his attack was unfair or not, we remark what Seneca thought philosophy ought to be doing, its function.

He clearly thought that its function is admonitory, hortatory, consolatory. It is to keep us on an even keel amidst the buffets and vicissitudes of fortune, so that neither trouble nor success can overturn us. In freeing us from the imperious sway of the passions, and from the worries of mundane affairs, philosophy can confer on us a godlike blessing: it can make us God's equals in this respect at least.

Philosophy, then, is truly a way of salvation, and the true philosopher is a saviour. This point of view is expressed most strikingly by Lucretius, the Roman disciple of the Greek Epicurus, in whose poem *On the Nature of the Universe*, written in the first century before Christ, the Epicurean philosophy is expounded with the passion of one who was convinced that he was the apostle of that good news for which the world was waiting. His eulogy of the Master, Epicurus, at the beginning of the work reads like a hymn of praise to some divine liberator – a liberator, paradoxically, from the shackles of religion, which, claims Lucretius, has been the author of far worse blasphemies than the nervous reader will meet in his pages: *his* poem will not command fathers to cut their daughters' throats in order to further a state enterprise, as the priests commanded Agamemnon on his way against Troy, 'when the Greek elite, the cream of mankind, befouled the altar of the Virgin abominably with the blood of Iphigeneia. As they draped her head with the sacrificial veil, which hid the trinkets the girl had put on, and when she saw the misery on her father's face as he stood by the altar, and realised that his assistants were trying to keep a blade hidden from her, and that the troops were crying as they looked at her, she sank to her knees and sought the earth in dumb terror. Nor was it of any avail to the child in her crisis that she had been the first to call the king 'father'; for they lifted her by the elbows and carried her trembling to the altar, not so that she might lead the joyful triumph of the bridal procession after a wedding-service, but that in the very flower of her maidenhood

she should be felled obscenely, a miserable victim of her own
father's hand – to give his armada a lucky send-off. Of such
cruelties have men been capable, under the suasion of religion.'

This is the supernatural tyranny whose stranglehold on man
Epicurus broke:

> When the life of man lay foul to see and grovelling upon
> the earth, crushed by the incubus of religion, which showed
> her face from the regions of heaven, lowering upon mortals
> with dreadful mien, a man of Greece it was who dared first to
> look her in the eye with his mortal eyes, who dared first
> stand forth to block her way: him neither the rumours of
> the gods nor thunderbolts checked, nor the sky with its
> muttered menaces, but rather they spurred on his mettlesome
> mind to be the first to break through the close-barred bolts
> of nature. And so it was that the lively force of his mind won
> its way, and he ranged on far beyond the fiery walls of the
> world, and in mind and spirit traversed the boundless whole;
> whence in victory he brings us tidings of what can come
> to be and what cannot, and in what way each thing has its
> power limited, and its deep-set boundary stone. And so it is
> the turn of religion to be cast beneath men's feet and
> trampled, and his victory has made us the equals of heaven.

Epicurus was actually called *Soter*, 'Saviour'. It was an epithet
given to gods, especially to Zeus and to Asclepius, the god of
healing. The title does not occur in the Homeric poems, though
there the gods often save men, from disaster or death. One
sense of the verb is that of 'rescuing from danger'. In this sense,
what the man is saved *from* is uppermost, what he is saved *to*
is usually only implied, but is sometimes stated – as when we
are told that the shipwrecked Odysseus, after being sea-battered
against rocks, was brought by a god safely, 'saved', to the mouth
of a smooth-flowing river. But it can also have the sense of
guarding or preserving a man (or thing) in his (or its) present
state of well-being.

At first the dangers from which the gods save one are physical
calamity and material misfortune; later, as Psyche grows to
maturity, they become more subtle: they threaten her with the
pains of hell, or block her as she reaches after heaven (however

'heaven' and 'hell' may be interpreted). It is thus that the mystery religions can be described as offering salvation, a share in the god's life in this world or the next, a realisation of the soul's divine potential.

The mystery cult of Dionysus, or Bacchus, it will be recalled, did this by merging the initiate with the god; the god possesses and fills him so that there is at-one-ment, and the initiate is then called by the god's name, *Bacchus*. The man's own mind, with its blinkered calculations of his petty mundane interests, is displaced by that of the god, who *inspires* him – literally, 'breathes into' him his own breath, spirit ('breath': in Latin *spiritus*, in Greek *pneuma*). Years ago the German scholar Erwin Rohde remarked how strange it was that a human being could thus surrender his or her personality to the experience of a communal frenzy; the phenomenon is less unfamiliar to the civilised now, in the age of the pop singer, than it was in Rohde's day, in the age of reason. And perhaps it would be more accurately put the other way round: the initiate was not losing a personality but finding one, in the person of the god which became his own (this may be the reason for the special appeal of the Dionysiac cult to women, in their own right mere 'second-class persons' in the philotimous system). The god provides the centre of gravity, the *point d'appui*, round which his devotee's *psyché* clusters. I am reminded that the Israelite kings have been described as being the 'soul' and 'character' of their people; this is a sort of parallel, but in the Dionysiac cult there was a tension between god and celebrant, whereby the latter was now possessed, now dispossessed, of the former, which marks it as a different stage in the emergence of individual personality.

With the appearance of the philosophical society, or societies, of the Pythagoreans (which I have described as an intellectual mystery religion, owing something in its inception to the Dionysiac), this *point d'appui* shifted from a sheer divinity, like Dionysus, to a divine *man*, Pythagoras – so that his adherents could be called 'Pythagoreans' – *Pythagoreioi*, 'Pythagoras's men', or even 'sons of Pythagoras'. Pythagoras, though a historical figure, quickly became a legend; later philosophies (Stoic and Cynic) took as their model a much remoter and more legendary 'divine man', Heracles (Hercules). Heracles's claim to historicity is tenuous in the extreme, but the important thing is that he was thought to have had a human existence, and to have been the embodiment of the Hesiodic virtue (*areté*) which Everyman can acquire by hard word: Hesiod himself described Heracles as 'most toilsome and best of men' – for by his labours he rid the world of fearsome monsters and so released mankind from their condition of nasty, brutish terror and made it possible for them to live tolerably. By the end of the fourth century BC the 'divine man', the saviour of his fellows, had become a figure not only historical but contemporary, recognisable in an outstanding thinker like Epicurus, or in a successful statesman or man of action.

By this time the original Pythagorean brotherhoods had died out, and the ecstatic cult of Dionysus had long been formalised and enervated, so that the later Dionysiac societies were little more than polite dining clubs. Something of the old enthusiastic style was maintained by the later oriental mysteries, particularly those of Isis and Mithras from Egypt and Persia, which captivated the populace of the western Mediterranean in the centuries just before and after the birth of Christ. We have a long and lyrical description of an initiation into the mystery of the goddess Isis by Apuleius, a Romanised African of the second century AD, in a passage of his novel which at this point is probably autobiographical (as well as allegorical). He tells how his hero, who has spent most of the book in the shape of an ass as the result of an unfortunate magical experiment, at last, by the grace of the goddess, regains his humanity – and regains it in an ennobled form. He devotes his life to his benefactress, and is initiated into her cult: he is 'reborn' to 'salvation', he says, after 'treading the confines of death and hell'; a hint at a ritual ordeal of 'death and resurrection'. This experience of 'putting off the old man and putting on the new' was uniquely elevating, but we are not told how the convert's day-to-day life was affected. Yet the waifs and strays of the philotimous system needed something more.

At the end of the fourth century BC *philosophy* had begun to try to do what Seneca said was its job: to offer vital aid and comfort to the individual, whose increasing sense of his individuation was bringing with it an increasing frustration at what appeared to him to be the dominant hostility of powers outside himself, imposing intolerable limitations on his divinity in the shape of misfortune, disease and death. (These powers did not have to be *super*natural: from the fifth century BC the words 'tyrant' and 'king' begin to take on nasty connotations which they did not have before.) This issued in a diffused anxiety of the spirit, to attain freedom from which was to attain salvation. It was this serenity of mind which the new philosophies promised to the individual.

The method of acquiring this serenity differed according to the diagnosis of the root-cause of the anxiety. For the Sceptics, late successors of Plato in the Academy, the cause of the trouble was intellectual: it was worry over metaphysical problems to which there can be no answer. They therefore tried to exorcise this worry by arguing equally cogently on both sides of the question, until it should be conceded that, as the true answer could not be demonstrated, the only rational thing was to suspend judgment about it. But much more popular than this thin and unappetising gruel were the systems of the Epicureans and the Stoics.

The Garden of Epicurus has already been mentioned. It was here, from the end of the fourth century BC, that Epicurus taught, and practised, his philosophy among the circle of his friends. He had himself been grounded in the atomic physics of Democritus, and on this physical theory he founded a moral doctrine.

Epicurus identified the thorn in the spirit of the New Man as concern about the blows which the whim of a higher power, a god or gods, might deal him either in this life or the next. But this concern he saw as caused by man's ascription to nature of man's own caprice and vindictiveness; by the assumption that the visitation of misfortune upon the righteous, while the wicked prosper, can only mean that the world is ruled by philotimous deities of the Homeric sort, implacable in venting their spite, even beyond the grave, on those they have taken against. He thought that this concern would be quelled if it could be shown that such a view of the gods was mistaken, and in addition that the soul is not immortal, but perishes with the body.

The gods, he argued, must, if they exist, be beings superlatively perfect, living perpetually in a state of the purest serenity. It would not be consistent with such bliss for them to have any truck with the affairs of our imperfect world. Nor is it necessary to postulate a divine power behind the workings of nature, all of which can be rationally explained without such an assumption, by the atomic theory.

Epicurus has been praised for his 'scientific materialism', and the praise may not be entirely unmerited, so long as we do not add 'and his concern for truth'. He adopted the Democritean physics, not because he thought it to be true, but because it suited his *moral* purpose: it eliminated divine control, or divine interference, from natural processes, and it entailed the mortality of the soul. If man had no fear of the gods, or of death, he held, we should have no need for natural science. His attitude was not really 'scientific' in a modern sense at all: if there were several 'naturalistic' explanations of a physical phenomenon, the truth of any of which would preclude supernatural action, it was sufficient for him to enumerate them. Which of them, if any, might be correct did not interest him: having heard them, you could take your choice. The important thing is to realise that there is no *need* to have recourse to 'divine direction' in order to explain it.

Democritus's system postulated, not a single stuff or 'substance' underlying all phenomena, but an infinite number of infinitesimal elementary solids, atoms (*atoma somata*, 'unsplittable bodies'), ever falling through infinite space. As they fall, they bump and jostle each other at random, their impacts being transmitted through the whole mass as if they were so many snooker balls knocking into each other; thus they group into larger agglomerates, sensible objects, which, by a process of 'survival of the fittest', come by chance in the course of infinite time to form again and again the sort of (apparently) orderly physical world we know – and to form us, living organisms with the capabilities to know it. And that by which we live and by which we know – our 'souls' and our 'minds' – are as material as everything else, formed of agglomerates of very fine atoms, which will disperse at our death like the crasser agglomerates which are our bodies. This is the triumph of Epicureanism – to show that 'death is nothing to us, and touches us not at all':

nil igitur mors est ad nos neque pertinet hilum, as Lucretius proclaimed. When we are, death is not, and when death is, we are not.

'That one was a god, a god, I tell you'; he had a divine majesty, who could divine the majestic secret of the universe. When Lucretius coursed through the immensity of space under Epicurus's guidance the scales fell from his mind's eyes, and he watched Nature everywhere busy at work. In this panorama nothing was hidden from him; he even saw the gods happy in their unruffled heaven, which he pictures in terms borrowed from Homer; but nowhere could he discern hell, which the proof of the soul's mortality had utterly erased:

> The gods in their majesty are revealed to my sight, and their tranquil abode, where they never feel the battering gale or the drenching rain or the icy edge of the white-falling snowflake, but they live under a pellucid sky which is forever cloudless and smiling and unstinting with its light. Nature meets their every need unasked, and at no time does any care detract from their peace of mind. On the other hand, though the opaque earth herself no longer hinders my vision of what passes underfoot throughout the void, the regions of hell nowhere appear. And hereupon I am seized with a pleasure which I must call divine, and my flesh thrills at my Master's power, who has so revealed Nature that no part of her is hidden from us.

However, though hell is dismissed, its pains are not. For Lucretius they are not hereafter, but here and now: they are allegories of the various anxieties which rack the hearts of living, unenlightened men. Tantalus, faint with fear at the rock which ever topples and threatens to fall and crush him, is the man oppressed by vain fears of the gods and tomorrow's mischances; Tityos, his entrails torn eternally by a vulture, stands for one whose desires are never satisfied; as for Sisyphus, ever trundling his boulder up the hill and never reaching the top but it evades him and goes bounding down again – we see him everywhere in the politician ambitious to scale the heights of an unattainable power; and the stories of infernal punishments and the demons who administer them symbolise the present action of the guilty conscience. 'Hell is the life of fools on earth' – fools, because they have their values wrong.

This may be called the negative side of Epicurus's teaching; and it must be admitted that it is the side which Lucretius stresses in his magnificent poem. But, having rid us of our inhibitions, how does the Master tell us to act? That we should act according to nature, and all things naturally seek pleasure and avoid pain: bearing this in mind, we should act always in the way we calculate will give us the greatest pleasure with the least pain.

Not surprisingly, Epicurus was charged with seeing man's highest good in sensual enjoyment, his *'summum bonum* in belly-cheer', so that his followers could be called 'pigs from Epicurus's sty'. But the free indulgence of the bodily appetites was certainly not the goal recommended to his disciples by one whose own moderate and frugal life matched his saying that 'he who is not content with little will never be content with much'. Intemperance suffers a reaction, and carnal pleasures are followed by a hangover. The greatest and most desirable pleasure is one which entails no ill consequences, and its savour is of the spirit rather than of the flesh: it is the pleasure engendered by the intercourse of friends.

It had been the Pythagoreans who had first banded together in groups of 'friends' whose bond was their common pursuit, not of some political or practical end, but of a certain philosophy and way of life. They are religious societies, and their meetings seem to have included a communal meal. Later stories made out this Pythagorean friendship to be something very special, forming ties even between Pythagoreans who were entire strangers to each other, as if they were members of some invisible church. Epicurean friendship was less mystical but more personal, and perhaps the more holy for that. Epicurus held friendship to be the greatest boon which wisdom bestows; though it has its origin in life's needs, friendship is more than a coincidence of self-interests, and is to be sought for its own sake; its value lies not so much in the aid which a friend gives us, as in the confidence that the aid is there if needed; the true friend is a 'second self', inasmuch as one will feel his pains and pleasures as if they were one's own (there's empathy for you!).

There were groups of his friends in other Greek cities, with whom Epicurus corresponded, but in the latter part of his life his headquarters was that garden in Athens, where periodically his little circle came together to enjoy the gay company of each other and the Master, even though he was suffering the anguish of a chronic disease. For Epicurus was not like Sam Johnson's college chum, who 'had tried to be a philosopher, but cheerfulness was always breaking in': he knew that laughter and wisdom are highly compatible. Another evidence of his kindly humanity is that slaves were admitted to his community as equals, and young women who would be termed 'call-girls' today, whose status as persons in Epicurus's Athens was not even second-class; a fact which of course was fruitful of snide comment from outside.

Epicurus said that the best way to mourn a dead friend was to treasure his memory; and his own memory was kept green by his followers through the regular celebration of his birthday and monthly dinners in the Garden (the expense of which the Master had arranged to defray by a legacy). Yet his cult was not confined to these, but spread after his death like wildfire; we hear that it took Italy by storm when it was introduced there in the second century BC. It went far to answer a need that men were feeling deeply; yet its joy was tinged with a sadness, typified by a phrase in Epicurus's final letter: 'I write to you on the happiest day of my life – the happiest, because it is the last.'

Quite different from the Epicureans in the tone and details of their system, but like them aiming to hearten and guide the individual in the trials of life's journey, were their contemporaries the Stoics. Their founder, the Cypriot Zeno, had come to Athens and taught there in the Colonnade of Many Colours (the *Stoa Poikile*, from which the name 'Stoic' was taken). Zeno's philosophy was, like that of Epicurus, entirely materialistic, in the sense that it made no fundamental distinction between the physical and the 'psychical'; it denied that 'soul' (*psyché*) was an entity different in kind from 'body' (or 'matter'), as Plato and the Pythagoreans would have it. Everything without exception is composed of the four elements which Empedocles had postulated – earth, water, air and fire; the last however having a special quality which links it with Heraclitus's basic fiery substance. For Zeno's elemental fire was not the fire in the grate (which is fire in its crudest form), but in its pure form so fine and subtle as to be invisible (this purity is manifested to the senses most worthily in the fire of the heavenly bodies); active, intelligent, ubiquitous, it is that which organises each body – what each one calls his 'mind'; and, as permeating the whole universe and organising it, 'holding it together', it is Creative Fire, the Divine Mind, God. As the Roman Stoic poet Manilius put it, in a passage already quoted, 'just as the physical world is a receptacle for divine Mind which suffuses and steers the whole, so our bodies too are the hospices of mind, which rules supreme and orders the whole man'. And as the parts of an individual organism co-operate for the benefit of the whole (the functional idea of *physis*, 'nature', again), so all the parts of the universe must be working together harmoniously for the common good. God is Nature, but Nature benevolent, provident and unerring; looked at in another way, he is Fate – not however a whimsical petty tyrant, dealing out fortune capriciously to individuals, but determining all for the good of all; a benevolent autocrat.

To be a virtuous man is to 'follow nature', but this rule has a different interpretation from that given it by the Epicureans: to the Stoic it meant, to surrender self-will to that portion of the universal god which speaks at the centre of one's own mind ('Fate drags the stubborn, but leads the meek'). This we can all do, whoever we are; virtue (*areté*) in no way depends on the accidents of outward circumstances, on health, or wealth, or high birth. Such accidents are in themselves neither good nor bad: they are 'indifferent', but they can be used well or ill according to the disposition of their possessor. Even life itself is not intrinsically good, but 'indifferent', and deliberately to put an end to one's life by one's own hand, should the burden of misfortune prove intolerable, may be an act not only blameless but laudable. This was a novel attitude to suicide, a deed which aroused horror and revulsion in classical Greeks, and which would have aroused surprise in Homer's pre-classical heroes, for whom it would have been an act not so much morally distasteful as almost inconceivable, except for one deranged by grief.

As the basic imperative of 'nature' appears to be *Survive!*, and as the minimal requirements for survival in terms of nutrition and protection from the elements are simple, it is not surprising that the Stoic's prescriptions for individual behaviour were austere. But it was an austerity ennobled by that extended conception of nature as a benevolent governor concerned for the general good of its entire realm; so the Stoic man of virtue will combine the least concern for himself and his means of survival with the greatest concern for the well-being of society, of which he is a part: he will exemplify that 'charity', or unselfish concern for others, which is first learned at home in the loving relationship of parents and children, then extended to neighbours and finally to all mankind (the real meaning of the much misused saying, 'charity begins at home'). Stoicism taught you unselfishness, but it was unselfishness tinged with superiority: it taught you also to be proud in your unselfishness.

The Stoics did not honour their founder with a status akin to that of divinity, as did the Epicureans. But Roman Stoics later came to see the incarnation of their ideal in a high-principled Roman statesman of the first century BC, the younger Cato. We possess a most interesting literary portrait of this man made a hundred years after his death, by the poet Lucan. Its interest lies in what it tells us of the spiritual longings of its author and like minds with his in the Rome of the mid-first century of our era. Its proper appreciation requires some knowledge of the poet's background, and we are fortunate in having more and better information about the short life of Lucan than we have about the life of almost any other ancient writer.

Born in AD 39 in the Spanish town of Cordova, he was the nephew of Seneca, that tutor of the emperor Nero whom we have already met, and one of the richest men in the Roman empire; nephew too of Gallio, the governor of the Roman province of Greece before whom Paul appeared in AD 52. His father was called perverse: wealthy enough to buy out the leaders of society, he yet preferred to remain on the sidelines, relishing this thought in comparative obscurity (this independent trait was to show in the son too).

As if it were not bad enough to be born into a family of such influence and affluence, the child Lucan was also endowed with a precocious brilliance. Charming his family first with infantile chatter, soon with learned epyllia, he went on as a student quickly to surpass his teachers, and to captivate the public with his poetic effusions. By the age of twenty he was admitted to the intimate circle of the emperor Nero himself, who was a practising artist in many fields – a composer of poems and libretti, ballet-dancer, lyrist and organist – and one of whose less reprehensible ambitions was to instil some aesthetic sense into his barbarous fellow-Romans. For a time all went well between the young Nero and the young Lucan; but both men were conceited, impetuous and innocent of self-criticism, and there can be no doubt which was the better poet. Estrangement followed, and the jealous emperor condemned Lucan to literary death, forbidding him to plead in the courts or to publish his poetry. Lucan retaliated with gibes and lampoons, finally joining some vacillating conspirators, whom he terrified with his brave and loud talk of exacting vengeance on the absurd tyrant's person. Their unmasking led to a bloodbath of suicides and executions, in which not only Lucan but his father and uncles perished.

Lucan was only twenty-five when he died, but his great work has survived. This was an epic poem, to challenge Virgil's *Aeneid*, on the civil war waged successfully a century before by Julius Caesar against the forces of republican Rome led by Pompey – the birthpangs of Imperial Rome. The author poses as a staunch republican, and, in spite of fulsome flattery of Nero at the beginning, hurls scathing invective at Caesar and the Caesarian dynasty – of which of course Nero was a member. But Lucan's bitterness against Caesar is less than his bitterness against the gods.

Lucan had already shown his self-confidence and independence of mind in several ways: his marriage had been a love-match, against the wishes of his father, his literary ambition was to supplant Virgil as Rome's national poet-laureate, his artistic pride would not be cowed even by the power of the emperor. Now, in his poem, he threw down the gauntlet to heaven.

The interesting thing about Lucan's uncle Seneca is, as I have put it, that he was an example of a philotimous man who hated

philotimia; the interesting thing about Seneca's nephew is that
he was furious with God for not existing – or, if he does exist,
for being such a contemptible sort of god, who could only make
a world in which death is the greatest boon, and in which a
tyrannic Caesar can overcome the forces of freedom. Lucan
sensibly did not import Homer's Olympian gods into this
historical epic, where their presence would have been patently
absurd, but he often speaks sarcastically of 'the gods' – or whatever it is that manages or mismanages the universe (if it is
anything but chance). It is true that Lucan had had a Stoic
tutor, and his noblest poetry is about the impersonal Stoic god
of universal nature, but it is the product of wistfulness rather
than of conviction. It is put into the mouth of one of his
characters, Cato. Lucan's regard is reserved for *men* who rise
above the gods: for Caesar (paradoxically), who browbeats them,
and for Cato, who is their moral superior.

Much as Lucan vilifies Caesar, painting him as a villain of the
blackest hue, without one redeeming feature, it is clear that he
felt a deep admiration, however grudging, for the man of action
who 'believed naught accomplished while aught remained un-
done'. Caesar dominates the poem, even when he is absent from
the stage, and his entrances electrify it. In the first book Lucan
gives an excellent vignette of him, comparing with his adversary,
the vain and flabby Pompey, resting on the laurels of past
achievements, Caesar's 'mettle which did not know how to stay
still', 'energetic and indomitable, answering with equal alacrity
the promptings of hope or of anger, snatching up the sword
without waiting for justification, always pushing his luck and
treading on the heels of his success; toppling any obstacle to his
way to the summit, and exulting in the ruin caused by his
passage; ashamed of nothing but of winning without a fight.' In
his troops he inspired a mixture of blind loyalty and superstitious
terror. Once when, driven too far, they turned mutinous, their
general's eye and a short speech were enough to quell them;
they were convinced that their own swords would leap from their
scabbards, willy-nilly, at Caesar's order.

The gods, who 'look after criminals, and can only visit their
anger on the unfortunate', were as much in awe of him as were
his men. Caesar had supreme confidence in his 'lucky star', and

reckoned that heaven had let him down, not if it did not answer, but if it did not *anticipate* his wish. After he had had a slight setback, the gods tried to creep back into his good books by granting him a series of successes. No wonder that his troops, when ordered by him to desecrate a holy place, preferred to risk heaven's anger rather than Caesar's!

If Caesar outdoes the gods by his self-confident audacity, Cato outdoes them by his calm virtue. He is the incarnation of the Stoic ideal man, compounded with the traditional old Roman virtues – virtues possessed in profusion by Romans long dead, but by live Romans not at all. His support makes the losing cause the better cause: 'The gods favoured the winning side, but Cato the losers.' Like Caesar, he is a man of action, but only when driven to action by deliberate choice and a sense of duty, not when driven, like Caesar, by passion, *thymos*. Cato's concern is always for the common good, never for his own. 'This was the code of conduct which stern Cato set himself to follow unswervingly: to observe moderation, always to judge the act by the intent, to follow Nature, to devote his life to his country. That he had been born to serve mankind, not himself, was his creed. Enough to quench the pangs of hunger was to him a banquet, a roof that could fend off the storm was as good as a palace; to him a hair shirt, such as Rome's founder had worn, was royal raiment. He knew the act of love only to have offspring: it was for Rome, for his country, that he married and had children. A worshipper of Justice, a devotee of decency however exacting, he did his duty for the good of all, not for some partisan benefit. In nothing that Cato did did self-seeking Pleasure sneak in and filch a share.'

The outbreak of civil war, when states tear out their own guts, distressed him exceedingly. In an extraordinary outburst, Lucan makes him pray that he might avert it by dying as a sacrificial victim to atone for the sins of both sides. He was under no illusions about either of the leaders: Pompey's motives were no better than Caesar's, and the battle was not to be between freedom and tyranny, but to decide which of them was to be tyrant of Rome, which of them was to be master of the mistress of the world. Like Brutus, he 'was not the enemy of Caesar or of Pompey, but would be the enemy of the victor'; reluctantly, he joined the republican side, to ensure that among the Pompeian forces there should be at least one *Roman*. That so holy a man as Cato was driven to taint himself with the abomination of civil war was a charge to be laid at the gods' door, not Cato's.

After the manner of the *Iliad*, where long sections are devoted to exemplifying the prowess of this hero or that, Lucan devotes a lengthy portion of his epic to 'the prowess of Cato'. But his hero excels, not in bravery and slaughter of the enemy, but in personal endurance of physical hardship and in concern for the well-being of his men. The scene is a forced march through the Libyan desert, wherein the foe is not Caesar but heat and thirst and venomous reptiles. These Cato's troops overcame, not by their leader's orders, but by his example. Always at the head of the column on the march, always at the rear of the queue for water at an oasis (except once, where it was thought to be poisoned), he yet was everywhere where he was needed, cheering the failing and by his mere presence giving the dying strength to meet death bravely.

In their journey they passed a temple which housed an oracle of the god Amon. One of Cato's lieutenants suggested that they stop to question it. Cato's lofty refusal, embodying the Stoic creed in a nutshell, is one of Lucan's finest passages:

What question would you have me ask? Whether I should prefer death in battle, a free man, to life under a tyrant? Whether mere living has any value in itself, or whether length of life makes any difference to its quality? Whether violence has any power to harm a good man, or Fortune's ugliest threats can bluff the virtuous? Whether failure matters, if the intention be good? We know the answers already, and the oracle will not drive the knowledge deeper home. We are all inseparable from the divine, and do nothing but God wills it, even if his temples give us no directions. The deity needs no voice to speak to us: the source and author of our being planted in us once for all at our birth all that we should know. Do you think that he chose these desert sands in which to bury the truth away, so that few would hear his message? Do you think that his dwelling-place is here rather than everywhere without and within us – in earth, sea, air and sky, and in the virtuous heart? Why look further for him? God is all that we see, all that we feel. Fortune-tellers are for the doubters, the perpetual worriers about tomorrow. *My* certainty I owe to no oracle, but to the certainty of death. The coward and the brave, both must die; this is God's edict, and it is enough for me.

This reply Cato uttered 'inspired by the deity enshrined in the oracle of his heart'; and he moved on, sparing the god's oracle the test which it would have met only with some feeble equivocation.

While conceding sublimity of sentiment to Stoicism, modern minds may be repelled by its lack of emotion, its in-turned 'apathy' and resignation to fate. Yet clearly Lucan – like many others – was fired by its ideals, even if he was far from embodying them in his own life. We may compare the feelings of the young man in a Greek comedy, who tells the audience of his conversion to philosophy with a religious enthusiasm:

Believe me, friends, I've been dead all my life till now. The beautiful, the good, the awesome and the bad were all one to me. Such was the darkness, you can call it, of my mind, which hid the truth about all these things and made it invisible to me. Now I've come here it's just as if I'd been ill and slept in the temple of Asclepius and the god had saved me and given me a new life from now on. I stroll about and have discussions and I use my mind. Such a dazzling sun has now risen for me as I never knew before: for the first time I am seeing you, my friends, in daylight, and this sky, this acropolis, this theatre.

The religious language is manifest: it is as if the young man has had a revelation from a god, through which he has been saved, reborn. The darkness of his soul has been illumined by a joyous inner light, which has transformed the way in which he sees the outer world. In other words, he has experienced *metanoia*, of which the customary translation, 'repentance', is an inadequate and rather misleading rendering, for the sense of the word covers not only a 'change of heart' but also a 'change of head', a basic shift in one's point of view of the world.

A surprising conjunction, this; the rapturous joy of the mystical experience hand-in-hand with the steely pessimism of the Stoic, or the gentle pessimism of the Epicurean. Then we remember that it is in the mouth of a character in a play; the voice of aspiration rather than of reality.

7

Lightning from Heaven

'The great Pan is dead!' cried the preacher, and he smote the lectern hard enough to waken the rooks from their siesta in the rectory elms.

Every Sunday I used to be marched from school what seemed many miles to church, but this is the only sermon I can remember. In it we heard Plutarch's story, from his essay on *Why the Oracles are now Silent*, of how, one summer evening in the reign of the Roman emperor Tiberius, a ship was coasting by a little island off western Greece, when those on board were startled to hear a loud voice calling 'Thamus! Thamus!' Now this was the name of the ship's captain. At first he did not respond, but when called a third time he answered. Then said the voice: 'When you come to Palodes, say that the great Pan is dead.' There was consternation on board, and debate about what was to be done. Finally, Thamus decided that, if the ship were under way passing Palodes, he would do nothing; but if it were becalmed then, he would obey the voice. Off Palodes the wind dropped, and Thamus announced: 'The Great Pan is dead!' Immediately was heard the sound of loud lamentation, as of an invisible multitude in mourning.

Plutarch's point was that even gods can die; the Reverend Mr Welland's, that Jesus's ministry dethroned the old gods.

> The oracles are dumm,
> No voice or hideous humm
>   Runs through the arched roof in words deceiving.
> *Apollo* from his shrine
> Can no more divine,
>   With hollow shriek the steep of Delphos leaving.
> No nightly trance, or breathed spell,
> Inspires the pale-ey'd priest from the prophetic cell.

The lonely mountain o're,
And the resounding shore,
    A voice of weeping heard, and loud lament;
From haunted spring, and dale
Edg'd with poplar pale,
    The parting Genius is with sighing sent,
With flowre-inwov'n tresses torn
The Nimphs in twilight shade of tangled thickets mourn.

Though the pagan divinities were to be pronounced diabolical
by an uncompromising church, this was no glib case of 'the
gods of one religion becoming the devils of its successor'. Something new did come into the world on the first Christmas Day,
which was to offer men's souls an alternative spring of energy
to that provided by *philotimia,* and which could aptly be allegor-
ised as defeating and routing the old, spent deities of the philotimous system.

Albert Schweitzer has said that the historical Jesus must
elude our researches; that he speaks individually, and presents
himself differently, to each one's heart; that, in effect, there are
as many Jesuses as there are men (or men who bother with
him at all). The professional historian may illuminate peripheral
circumstances but can never recapture the whole person. This
of course is true of any biography, but it is uniquely difficult in
the case of Jesus, where the scholar is confronted at the outset
with the problem of what criteria of truth he is to apply. Ordinarily the historian's ultimate criterion must be probability –
what he thinks is the most likely reconciliation of his varied evidence; and this assessment must be tempered by his own experience and by the tacit assumptions or prejudices inherent in
the climate of his intellectual milieu. His assessment is therefore
highly subjective: he cannot set up an experiment in the
laboratory to test his hypothesis, as a scientist would. Quite
different views of what is historically probable would be held
by a medieval monk, accustomed to expect nocturnal demons in
the reredorter, and a twentieth-century scientific atheist. Anyway,
how can the conscientious historian start to deal with what is
claimed to be an *unparalleled* event, such as the Incarnation?
The very basis of his methodology is that there are *no* unique

events – that the unknown must always be explicable in terms of the known (or the untried in terms of the tried). Is he then to leave it alone? Hardly; that would entail meek obedience to anyone who might say, 'Boys, this is hallowed ground, a place on its own: go away and mess up somewhere else.'

The dilemma is a real one. Even so, granting that the historian must be guided by his view of what *probably* occurred, what *actually* occurred may have been the improbable. There will always be room, as well as need, for faith; faith, and wariness of those who neither enter into the kingdom of heaven themselves nor allow others to enter therein.

'As many Jesuses as there are men who bother about him.' Ever since I can remember, he has bothered me; in my life singularly fortunate amidst the huge miseries of a world which man has cruelly misshaped, self-indulgent, prone to the conviction that what I want to believe must be true, he has bothered me like hell. The light was there, shining through the marvellous language of the Authorised Version of the gospels, still shining through the barriers of translation and inevitable mistranslation, distortion and deliberate interpolation. I cannot believe that Jesus was a myth, and never existed; I cannot believe that he was really a committee; I cannot believe that he was a half-crazy tool of Joseph of Arimathea and a group of *illuminati;* and I cannot at all believe that the mushrooming of Christian societies all over the world is accountable to a toadstool (a recent theory has it that the originator of Christianity was the hallucinogenic fungus *amanita muscaria,* the Fly Agaric). I do believe that in him was resolved that internal tension divorcing the human from the divine which for the past five hundred years Mediterranean man had been experiencing ever more sharply; that in him Psyche reached maturity, or was 'reborn', and God's love was manifested in a shape that the world had not so far seen.

More than three hundred years before him the conquests of Alexander the Great had carried the Greek language, and with it Greek culture and Greek values, across the Middle East as far as India, and southwards through Palestine to Egypt – in the first century BC even the Parthians, about the valley of the Euphrates beyond the frontier of the Roman empire, had a taste for the plays of Euripides. In the second century Jerusalem itself had been affected by the rage for Hellenism – or infected by it, as it seemed to stricter Jews who reacted sharply to such foreign ways in some of their compatriots. In Jesus's time Jerusalem still had its sympathisers with Hellenism in the wealthy and powerful Sadducees.

By now Greek had become the common tongue of the countries bordering the eastern Mediterranean. Whether Jesus himself knew Greek has been disputed, but he grew up in Galilee, the 'circle of the Gentiles', no cultural backwater but an international highway, near Gadara with its three theatres and other Greek-speaking towns of the Decapolis. It is true that Jesus seems deliberately to have avoided such places – he was addressing himself in the first place to his own people – and, even if he did understand the language, it cannot be supposed that he was educated in Greek literature. But the ambience of Greek culture, and the tensions which the development of that culture had produced, were all around him; percolations by now into the common spiritual atmosphere. This was the context that called forth the gospel. Granted that the good news was addressed to Israel, it was to the Hellenised peoples that it really spoke. The Greco-Roman world was to be israelised, and the Gentiles were to be included in the People of God.

Exact historians tell us that Jesus was born in BC 4 or perhaps slightly earlier – a freak of chronology to be laid at the door of a monk, one Denis the Midget, who established the date of our Christian era. But St. Luke has a worse shock in store: Jesus was born thirty years before Christ – if Christ's birth is equated with the baptism of Jesus by John.

Something crucial happened then. Of Jesus's life before that point we are told almost nothing: in Luke's phrase, up to then he was increasing in wisdom and in years, and in favour in the eyes of God and man. Within and without, pressure was building up. The Baptist himself felt it: 'I baptise you,' he told his congregation, 'with water; but one mightier than I cometh, the latchet of whose shoes I am not worthy to unloose: he shall baptise you with the Holy Ghost and with fire.' For Jesus, this was the point of resolution: as he emerged from the water of John's baptism, he felt the breath (*pneuma*) of God entering him, in the inspiration of the Holy Ghost, and saw it in the form

of a dove descending upon him from heaven, and he heard a
voice saying, 'This is my beloved son, in whom I am well pleased.'

The nuclear sense of the verb (*agapan*) from which *agapetos*,
'beloved', is derived is 'to regard as the apple of one's eye', 'to
take particular joy in', and to treat accordingly. It is used of a
parent's feeling for his child (especially an only child – something unique), of a lover's feelings for the beloved, of the artist's
for his creation. The related noun *agapé* – uncommon in pagan
Greek – is specifically used of that shape of love newly manifested in Jesus Christ, which as a spring of an individual's
action is the reverse of *philotimia*, 'love of one's own status': for
agapé confers *timé*, 'value' or 'honour', on others, it does not
seek *timé* from others (giving being more blessed than receiving);
and it negates the grading of people into 'superior' and 'inferior'
which is the essence of the philotimous system. This was a point
which the disciples of Jesus were slow to take; their obtuseness
was rebuked in their own philotimous terms. 'He asked them,
What was it that ye disputed among yourselves by the way? But
they held their peace: for by the way they had disputed among
themselves, who should be the greatest. And he sat down, and
called the twelve, and saith unto them, If any man desire to be
first, the same shall be last of all, and servant of all. And he
took a child, and set him in the midst of them: and when he
had taken him in his arms, he said unto them, Whosoever shall
receive one of such children in my name, receiveth me: and
whosoever shall receive me, receiveth me not, but him that sent
me.' The keys of the kingdom of heaven are here symbolised in
the persons of the lowliest servant, the doormat of the philotimous, and the child, who is not yet bemused by the spell of
philotimia.

Without *agapé* the person is a mere hollow mask, echoing the
lines of its set piece, its role, a 'sounding brass or tinkling cymbal'
in Paul's famous words, answering only to some external stimulus.
Agapé is the disposition (*thelema*) of God the Father; it is that
which moves the heavenly kingdom, and which can move earth,
if earth will accept the gift: 'Thy Kingdom come. Thy will
(*thelema*) be done, in earth, as it is in heaven.'

But with the realisation, or incarnation, of *agapé* something
else happened also: its opposite entered the realm of psychic

possibility. *Corruptio optimi pessima,* corrupt the best and you have the worst: *philotimia,* that general concern for status which motivated worldly societies now acquired a new, personal dimension, that of 'spiritual pride', the desire to subordinate other persons to one's own person, to make their selfhood dependent on one's own; a sublime sin, the sin which was to be called the cause of Satan's fall. 'I saw Satan fall as lightning from heaven', Jesus told his disciples; Satan, the Accuser of man before God but till now a heavenly angel of God none the less, was henceforth to be God's adversary, Anti-God, and salvation and damnation were to take on a deeper meaning. It was the inner promptings of this Anti-God which Jesus rejected in the wilderness, when he was tempted to use his spiritual powers to gain temporal dominion over men by putting himself in the place of God. 'And the devil, taking him up into an high mountain, shewed unto him all the kingdoms of the world in a moment of time. And the devil said unto him, All this power will I give thee, and the glory of them: for that is delivered unto me; and to whomsoever I will I give it. If thou therefore wilt worship me, all shall be thine.' Satan is cast as 'the lord of this world', the arch-potentate, because he is 'a liar, and the father of' lying; and the puppets of the philotimous way follow appearances rather than reality, they 'clean the outside of the cup and of the platter, but within they are full of extortion and excess', and are like 'whited sepulchres, which indeed appear beautiful outward, but are within full of dead men's bones'.

Philotimia had been given a new and terrible aspect; what might be called its perfected form – which the kindly Christian father Origen thought had never been exemplified, even in the devil, who would himself be saved in the end. Under the old dispensation the individual could be a failure in the sense that he could fail in his philotimous role in society – he could prove to be a faulty puppet; but under the new dispensation of (self-chosen) 'self-fulfilment' it was impossible to be a failure – one cannot fail to be one's self; but, if the choice has been wrong, success could be ghastly.

This spiritual power, this authority which men remarked in Jesus, so affected those who saw and heard him that some experienced that conversion or refocusing of the soul called *metanoia,* translated as 'repentance' in the Authorised Version; and others cried out in anguished protest at his mere approach, as did the demoniacs. 'What have we to do with thee, Jesus, thou son of God? art thou come hither to torment us before the time?' – before he had said a word or done a thing. The converted saw the world in a new light, and their experience showed outwardly in the disappearance of physical ailments from which they might be suffering, and inwardly in the wiping-away of 'sins' they had committed in their former unenlightened state. Jesus himself deprecated the importance which the populace (not surprisingly) attached to these miracles of healing, which were not his main concern, but a by-product of men's reaction to him; and it is significant that they were not much in evidence when he was in Nazareth where his fellow-townsmen greeted the carpenter's son's teachings with raised eyebrows.

Jesus's main concern was the coming of the Kingdom of God, when the *agapé* of the Father would be echoed and manifested in His children on earth, and this he proclaimed in homely parable and forceful paradox. This kingdom will not be a visible one, it will display no imperial apparatus like an earthly government; it will be invisible, in the hearts of men. 'When he was demanded of the Pharisees, when the kingdom of God should come, he answered them and said, The kingdom of God cometh not with observation: neither shall they say, Lo here! or, Lo there! for, behold, the kingdom of God is within you.' Like a seed, it is implanted in the soul in a moment; but then, like a seed, it grows slowly until it reaches the dimensions of a great tree; or its action may be compared to that of a little yeast in much flour. 'Another parable put he forth unto them, saying, The kingdom of heaven is like to a grain of mustard seed, which a man took, and sowed in his field, which indeed is the least of all seeds: but when it is grown it is the greatest among herbs, and becometh a tree, so that the birds of the air come and lodge in the branches thereof'; and 'the kingdom of heaven is like unto leaven, which a woman took, and hid in three measures of meal, till the whole was leavened'. These parables are equally applicable to the process of growth within the individual *psyché* and to the process of spread from individual to individual within a community. To put it in a more modern, and less savoury, parable: it is like a germ which is passed on from person to person, and affects the susceptible; we catch it from each other.

To be one of the Kingdom is to enter into 'eternal life', that fuller, more robust and personal life which the mysteries had adumbrated and the young convert to philosophy had glimpsed; to have taken the first step on this path is to receive the promise of more, whereas not to have done so is all-stultifying. 'For whosoever hath, to him shall be given, and he shall have more abundance: but whosoever hath not, from him shall be taken away even that he hath.' But how does one qualify for entry?

'Except a man be born again,' said Jesus to Nicodemus the Pharisee, 'he cannot see the kingdom of God.' 'Nicodemus saith unto him, "How can a man be born when he is old? can he enter a second time into his mother's womb, and be born?" Jesus answered, "Verily, verily, I say unto thee, Except a man be born of water and of the Spirit, he cannot enter into the kingdom of God".' The operation of the Holy Spirit, *Pneuma*, entering into the man makes him anew, it is as if his old self is washed away; he has undergone the baptism of Christ. But the advent of the Spirit cannot be commanded; no formula, magical or scientific, can bind it; it is as free as the wind's breath. 'The wind bloweth where it listeth, and thou hearest the sound thereof, but canst not tell whence it cometh, or whither it goeth: so is everyone that is born of the Spirit.'

As the Holy Ghost does not command, so it does not answer commands; but it will answer requests. 'Ask, and it shall be given you; seek and ye shall find; knock and it shall be opened unto you: for every one that asketh receiveth; and he that seeketh findeth; and to him that knocketh it shall be opened.' Those who want to find the right way with the force of a physical longing will succeed. 'Blessed are they which do hunger and thirst after righteousness: for they shall be filled.' But the desire must be unqualified, without reservations. 'No man, having put his hand to the plough, and looking back, is fit for the kingdom of God.' And practise that which in the fulness of the Kingdom, will spring from *agapé* unrehearsed: be as concerned for your neighbour's good as if it were your own, even if he is your enemy – and your neighbour (as the parable of the Samaritan shows) is anyone with whom you have dealings, even the most casual passer-by; so the love of your neighbour, whom you have seen, may lead you to the love of God, whom you have not seen, and the one love will enhance and complete the other. Practise also the philotimous vices: spiritual humility, willing service, gentleness, pity, pacification. 'Blessed are the poor in spirit: for theirs is the kingdom of heaven. Blessed are the meek: for they shall inherit the earth. Blessed are the merciful: for they shall obtain mercy. Blessed are the peacemakers: for they shall be called the children of God.' Do this, and you will be doing the 'righteous' thing – what it is right and proper for a *man* to do – and you may earn yet another blessing: 'Blessed are they which are persecuted for righteousness' sake: for theirs is the kingdom of heaven.' Not surprisingly, those who have the philotimous virtues – wealth, family, office – will find it most difficult to enter the kingdom: they will hardly reject the standards which they already successfully meet.

According to another Beatitude, 'Blessed are the pure in heart: for they shall see God.' It is not outward, formal purity that matters, but the inward truth. Jesus addresses the innermost *psyché;* it is the cast of soul that counts, its intentions, rather than actions. 'Ye have heard that it was said by them of old time, Thou shalt not commit adultery: but I say unto you, That whosoever looketh on a woman to lust after her hath committed adultery with her already in his heart.' In like manner a man really taints himself, not with extraneous physical dirt, or the formally unclean, but with his own psychic vomit, as when his self-love (or self-hatred) issues in words calculated to undermine his fellow-man's self-confidence, and to belittle him. 'Not that which goeth into the mouth defileth a man; but that which cometh out of the mouth, this defileth a man.' 'Whosoever shall say to his brother, Thou fool, shall be in danger of hell fire' – for he is destroying the other's self-respect, diminishing him as a person. Of course in the philotimous society one is doing this continually almost as a reflex action; but if one *realises* what one is doing, if it is part of a deliberate policy, then it is time to beware, and consider one's own peril.

Although Jesus's teaching is pre-eminently about persons in their relationships with each other ('Where two or three are gathered together in my name, there am I in the midst of them'), and the kingdom of heaven is not to be enjoyed in solitude, his morality is not a social morality, which depends for its enforcement on the restraints of law or on social approval or disapproval, but an intimately personal one. It is the disposition (*thelema*) of one's own *psyché* that matters, and it is there, in the *psyché*, that the consequences of that disposition will be felt by the individual. It may be long before the secrets of the heart are revealed, even to one's self; how much less can we know of the hearts of others! For their apparent shortcomings, then, ready complacence; for our own, castigation and correction. 'Judge not, that ye be not judged. For with what judgment ye judge, ye shall be judged; and with what measure ye mete, it shall be measured to you again. And why beholdest thou the mote that is in thy brother's eye, but considerest not the beam that is in thine own eye?'

Jesus aimed to change individuals in society, to substitute *agapé* for *philotimia* in them as their spring of action; he showed no desire to dismantle or transform the *machinery* of the society he knew. Changes in worldly society would be induced by individual *metanoia,* rather than the other way about. 'Render unto Caesar the things which are Caesar's, and unto God the things that are God's'; and Jesus was well aware of the adverse comment caused by his associations with tax-gatherers, the *publicani*, those most hateful representatives of the foreign oppressor. Any temporal society—that is, all societies, for all societies function within the framework of time – will have imperfections, as a harsh matter of fact, though they are not to be excused. 'Woe unto the world because of offences! for it must needs be that offences come; but woe to that man by whom the offence cometh!'

'Lay not up for yourselves treasures upon earth, where moth and rust do corrupt, and where thieves break in and steal: but lay up for yourselves treasures in heaven, where neither moth nor rust doth corrupt, and where thieves do not break through nor steal: for where your treasure is, there will your heart be also.' If Christ is made the focal point or gravitational centre for the personality, the man will be 'laying up treasures for himself in heaven'; he will be partaking in that 'eternal life' which Christ mediates, and will reach the stage at which he has no more need of 'heroes', 'focal points' or 'gravitational centres' because he will be complete ('perfect', as the Authorised Version has it: 'Be ye perfect, even as your Father which is in heaven is perfect'; 'self-fulfilled', perhaps, in modern idiom). He too will have become a 'son of God', as Jesus Christ, the 'first-born of the Father', gave all men the power to be. But to centre on ephemeral *philotimia* means decay, death and the rubbish-heap; it has not even the terrible distinction reserved for that spiritual, Satanic, *philotimia*, whose victory in the *psyché* is 'eternal death' and whose portion is the undying worm.

By mediating for us in time and space this aspect of God's love, Jesus Christ opened a new possibility for all men. It is to this that I take that strange text to refer, 'In my Father's house are many mansions . . . I go to prepare a place for you. And if I go and prepare a place for you, I will come again, and receive you unto myself; that where I am, there may ye be also.' There is something of a pun in the word translated in the Authorised Version as 'mansions': it can mean a 'room' in a house (which of course can be prepared for a guest), or a 'staging-post' in a journey. Jesus Christ by his life 'realised' a stage in Psyche's eternal journey, and therefore established that stage's existence, made it accessible ('prepared a place') for those who follow him, into which they will enter when it dawns on them what sort of a person he is. It is as God most perfectly demonstrated in human form that Jesus Christ claimed to be the way, the truth and the life, and said that 'No man cometh unto the Father, but by me'. The abandonment of the old, philotimous, standards – the standards of 'the world' – is a kind of death of the soul, necessary before it can be 'reborn in Christ': 'Whosoever will save his life shall lose it: but whosoever will lose his life for my sake, the same shall save it. For what is a man advantaged, if he gain the whole world, and lose himself, or be cast away?'

Even in his lifetime Jesus was an enigma; his own disciples could not make him out. He could not be docketed, he fitted nowhere. 'The foxes have holes, and the birds of the air have nests; but the Son of Man hath not where to lay his head.' Society had to kill him, as Australian aborigines killed the unclassifiable stranger, and the Athenians killed the irritating

Socrates; and philotimous society, whose values he had turned upside down, had to kill by a particularly nasty and ignominious death one who, on top of everything else, made claims which, measured by its own yardstick, were outrageous and frightening. The mockery, the crown of thorns, the cross were the inevitable end of the story. Inevitable, but not the end.

Epilogue

So, by the process which I have called *psychopoeia*, 'soulmaking', Psyche has reached a stage where she has earned her name and is fully-fledged; where, by her emergence into full self-consciousness, or the consciousness of what theologians have called 'the ground of being', she is confronted with the choice of imitating Christ or aping God. She now breathes an unfamiliar ether, superimposed upon, but not displacing, that social atmosphere in which she was nurtured; an ether in which her new freedom of individuality and choice will carry with it the gravest *personal* consequences, for she will have it in her, if she chooses, to be the deity, creator and inhabitant of her own universe.

Matters have moved out of the realm of the perceptible or the conceivable, into a crepuscular *intermundium* where one can only try to express the inexpressible by recourse to the machinery of the Platonic myth – though the word 'myth' in this context with its suggestion of fiction or falsehood, is rather unhappy. Plato used the form especially in discoursing about the *psyché*, or soul, or 'moral self', where it would be silly to suppose that anyone thought he could be telling the literal truth, but where he might be telling 'something like the truth'; where finality is not attainable, but a kind of wholeness is. The reader has already met in these pages some quotations from Plato's most famous myth about the destiny of the soul, the vision of Er, and I conclude with a major literary trespass, an extension of that vision.

'You have asked, Glaucon, about Er the Pamphylian, who when out of the body had a vision of the fate of souls, what other sights he saw which it was too long to tell the other day in our discussion about justice.

'He said that he was taken to a high place by one of grave and calm aspect, who told him "Thus far you have seen a part: now see the whole"; and he said that what Er was now to witness, as in a dramatic allegory, was the manner of the soul's coming-to-be and its determinations. When this was said, Er looked and saw below him four highways, from the south, the west, the north and the east, meeting at the centre in a crossroads. The highways were separated from each other, in the south-easterly quarter by fire, in the south-westerly by earth, in the north-westerly by air, and in the north-easterly by water. The parts in the south lay in semi-darkness, to the north they were illuminated by an ever-increasing light.

'Moving along the highway from the south, between the fire and the earth, were myriads of figures, of indistinct shape at first, but as they approached the crossroads he could discern them as having the shape of men. Yet, until they reached the crossroads, they appeared to be featureless, whether because of the darkness or for some other reason.

'When they emerged at the crossroads he could see, though not clearly, that they each had a face. But he noticed that many, before they reached the crossroads, had turned aside and sat down, as if wearied. Those who went forward hesitated at the parting of the ways for a shorter or longer time, as if in doubt by which road to proceed. Then, cheerfully or sadly, they set off, some to the east, others to the north, and yet others towards the west.

'Then he who stood by said to Er: "The darkness you see is mortal life, through which everything that comes to be must pass. The light is life eternal, towards which each thing that comes to be is moving. The road over which they pass in the darkness is bounded for them by the element of fire, the impulse (*thymos*) which moves them towards individuation, and by earth, the self-regard (*philotimia*) which moves them in their relation with others. Between these they are guided forward into the light of the life eternal at the crossroads. It is at this point, and not before, that they receive souls, being as it were born again.

' "In the light of the life eternal the elements of mortal life are transmuted into their opposites, the fire of *thymos* into air (*pneuma*), which is the urge towards the godhead, and the earth of *philotimia* into the water of *agapé*, the love of others. Those who suffer a complete rebirth, both of whose elements are transmuted into their opposites, proceed at once along the road to the north, and are safe. But those whose rebirth is defective, because one or other of their mortal elements is not transmuted into its opposite, proceed along the road to the east or to the west. He whose self-regard is transmuted into a love for others, but whose *thymos* is not transmuted, travels along the road to the east between the fire and the water, towards another coming-to-be in mortal life. He whose *thymos* is transmuted into *pneuma*, an urge towards the godhead, but whose self-regard is not transmuted into love for others, travels along the road to the west between the earth and the air, which leads to hell. But any who succeed in repairing the defect of their rebirth are instantly transported to the point on the road to the north corresponding to the distance they had travelled on the road to the east or to the west."

'When he had ceased saying this he turned Er about, and showed him another spectacle, of a great sphere whose surface was constantly erupting in protuberances, like the surface of some thick liquid boiling. Some of the protuberances rose but a little way above the surface before falling back into it, others rose higher like pinnacles, while some of these rose so high that the tips of the pinnacles bent backwards towards the surface of the sphere. When this happened, according to Er's relation it was a strange thing to see: for at a certain point flashes of light began to pass between the tip of the pinnacle and the surface of the sphere towards which it inclined, like a continual passage of lightning between sky and earth. But in such cases the outcomes were different: for Er remarked that some pinnacles ceased emitting flashes and, retracting themselves, collapsed back into the surface through their base. But the remainder became detached from the surface at their base, and for a time had a semblance of separate spheres, connected now to the surface through the passage of light which passed from them to it and back again. These terminated in one of two ways: either they merged into the surface of the great sphere through the column of light by which they were connected to it; or the column was severed, and they floated away independently.

'After gazing at this sight in silence for some time, Er asked his companion its meaning. "The great sphere," replied the other, "represents the one God. Though he is imaged as a sphere, He is unextended in space or time, the eternal ground of all being. Poets have described Him as Love, and in this they are not far wrong. But as Love unextended could only be self-love, and God rejects this, He divides Himself up, and this division is a continual coming-to-be and passing-away of entities in space and time, in which His nature appears under various names: as the attraction of mass for mass it is *baros*, gravity, as the hunger of one thing for another it is *epithymia*, as the desire for physical union *eros*, as familial affection *storgé*, as friendship *philia*, as universal love *agapé*. Creation, then, which is infinite in its variety, has no beginning and no end, is the obverse of eternity and the earnest that God rejects self-centred love. Space and time are imaged here by the surrounds of the sphere, and God's division of Himself in creation by the protuberances which rise from the surface of the sphere into the surrounds.

' "Those protuberances which you have seen to rise but little from the surface of the sphere, or into erect pinnacles, represent creatures with little, or no, self-consciousness. They correspond to the figures on the highway from the south, who never reached the crossroads. Their re-absorption into the eternal takes place without joy or terror, as they have not acquired souls. The acquisition of soul is represented by the flashing light from those pinnacles which have curved back towards the surface, when they face the eternal from which they have sprung, and become conscious of the conflict within themselves, the same conflict between self-love and love for others which God has resolved in Himself by the act of creation.

' "The pinnacles which ceased to emit flashes and were re-absorbed into the great sphere through their base are those who, with their souls, acquired love of others but not of God. They have accomplished the road to the east, and are re-absorbed – not without terrible visions, if they bethink themselves that they are suffering an irremediable loss; if not, not. For those pinnacles which were severed at the base, and whose connection with the great sphere thereafter was through the light of their souls, the outcome is decided by the resolution of the conflict between self-love and the love of others. Those who, seduced by hatred, falsehood and ugliness, have moulded their souls about barren self-love and completed the journey to the west have their reward: they become the god of their own separate universe, to people it forever with their own creations, such as they may be. But those whose souls, accompanied by love of others, truth and beauty, traverse the highway to the north, rejoin the God they adore as in a joyous homecoming, to be thenceforth His coadjutors in shaping the glories of His creation." '

References

Page 5. *Thomas Hanna*: the case was investigated by Drs Boris Sidis and S. Goodhart, and quoted by William McDougall (*An Outline of Abnormal Psychology*, pp. 484f.) (Methuen, 1926).

Page 6. *The Trickster*: see Mary Douglas, *Purity and Danger*, p. 79 (Routledge & Kegan Paul, and Praeger, 1966).

Page 7. *Iris Murdoch*: see *The Sunday Times* of 17/5/64.
J. A. C. Brown: in *Techniques of Persuasion*, pp. 212ff. (Penguin Books, 1964). I thank Mrs Hedy Brown for permission to quote from this work.

Page 14. *The Listener*: for 16/1/69, p. 67. I thank Dr Gertrude Keir for permission to quote from her report.

Page 22. *Ralph Linton*: in *The Study of Man*, p. 124 (Peter Owen, 1965).

Page 36. *Tale of Herodotus*: trans. George Rawlinson (slightly adapted) (Dent & Dutton, *Everyman's Library*, 1910).

Page 57 *Monoklissia*: see *The Times* of 10/1/63.

Page 59. *Frazer*: in *The Golden Bough*, vol. 3 (*Taboo and the Perils of the Soul*, p. 113) (Macmillan, 1911).

Page 82. *Er's story* is told as a myth by Plato in the tenth book of his *Republic*.

Page 85. *S. Baring-Gould*: in *A Book of Folklore*, p. 198 (Collins, n.d.).
Robert Burton: in *The Anatomy of Melancholy*, vol. 1, p. 192 (Dent & Dutton, *Everyman's Library*, 1932).

Page 86. *Addlers and menters*: see T. Keightley, *Fairy Mythology*, p. 308 (Bohn, 1850).
Benvenuto Cellini: from *The Life of Benvenuto Cellini*

(trans. by Anne Macdonnell, introduction by Wm. Gaunt; Dent & Dutton, *Everyman's Library*.)

Page 87. *G. N. M. Tyrrell*: in *Apparitions*, p. 147 (Duckworth, 1953).
John Lawson: in *Modern Greek Folklore and Ancient Greek Religion*, p. 131 (Cambridge University Press, 1910).
C. D. Broad: in *Lectures on Psychical Research*, p. 167 (Routledge & Kegan Paul, and Humanities Press, 1962).

Page 90. '*O nobly-born*': see W. Y. Evans-Wentz, *The Tibetan Book of the Dead*, p. 148 (Oxford University Press, 1949).

Page 91. *Certain mouths of hell*: R. Burton, *The Anatomy of Melancholy*, vol. 2, p. 41.

Page 92. *A perpetual snowstorm*: see G. G. Coulton, *Five Centuries of Religion*, vol. 1, pp. 446f. (Cambridge University Press, 1929).
H. H. Price: in *Proceedings of the Society for Physical Research*, vol. 50 (Jan. 1953). I thank Professor Price for permission to quote from his address.

Page 94. *C. D. Broad*: in *Lectures on Psychical Research*, p. x.

Page 102. *D. R. Stuart*: in *Epochs of Greek and Roman Biography*, pp. 127ff. (Biblo & Tannen, 1967).

Page 103. *Nesca Robb*: in *Neoplatonism of the Italian Renaissance*, p. 215 (Allen & Unwin, 1935).

Page 121. *Hippocrates*: see *The Sacred Disease*, chaps 2 and 4 (trans. W. H. S. Jones, vol. 2 of Loeb *Hippocrates*; Heinemann, and Harvard University Press, 1952).

Page 124. *One Greek at least*: his story is told by me in my *Aristeas of Proconnesus* (Oxford University Press, 1962).

Page 134. *The Israelite kings*: cf. S. Mowinckel, *He that Cometh*, pp. 69ff. (trans. G. W. Anderson; Blackwell, 1959).